HER APRIL DAYS

by

MRS ROBERT HENREY

LONDON
J. M. DENT & SONS LTD

All rights reserved
Printed in Great Britain
by Biddles Ltd, Guildford, Surrey
and bound at the
Aldine Press · Letchworth · Herts
for
J. M. DENT & SONS LTD
Aldine House · Albemarle Street · London
First published 1963
Second impression 1976

ISBN: 0 460 03536 3

HER APRIL DAYS

Thou art thy mother's glass, and she in thee
Calls back the lovely April of her prime.

SHAKESPEARE

MADELEINE HENREY

Event	Book	Date
Birth	THE LITTLE MADELEINE	Aug 13 1906
My father (Milou) b. 1873, dies	ditto	Apr 9 1921
Arrive alone aged 15 in London	ditto	Nov 1921
Mother (Matilda) follows		1922
Convent at Tooting	AN EXILE IN SOHO	1922
I work in a Soho newspaper shop	JULIA AND OTHERS	1922–3
Shopgirl at Galeries Lafayette	JULIA	1923–4
Typist to a silk merchant in City		1924
ditto at Gaumont, Denman St, Piccadilly		1925
I go with my mother to Paris to learn hairdressing	THE LITTLE MADELEINE	1925
I work in Coventry Street	A GIRL AT TWENTY	1926
Manicurist at the Savoy Hotel	MADELEINE GROWN UP	Feb–Dec 1927
First taken to Brentford to meet my future parents-in-law	GREEN LEAVES	1927
I fall ill and am sent by Robert to Pau		1928
Return in November—wedding at St George's, Hanover Square	MADELEINE GROWN UP	Dec 1 1928
We take an apartment in Beauchamp Place, Knightsbridge		1929
Effie and Burr leave Brentford and go to Godalming	GREEN LEAVES	1930
Girl diarist on London evening paper	ditto	1930–8
I buy the farm in Normandy		1937
Bobby born on the farm	MADELEINE YOUNG WIFE *Part One*	June 26 1939
Flee from the farm before advancing German army and return to London leaving Matilda on the quay	LONDON UNDER FIRE *and* MADELEINE YOUNG WIFE	1940
Burr dies at Godalming during the great raid on the City	GREEN LEAVES	Dec 31 1940
I return to Paris alone to find Paris just liberated—and my farm a scene of murder and desolation	LONDON UNDER FIRE *and* MADELEINE YOUNG WIFE *Part Two*	1945
Effie (b. May 15 1865) dies	GREEN LEAVES	1946
My mother (b. 1886) dies	HER APRIL DAYS	May 1962

I

SPRING had come round again. To be exact this was the first week in April—the year was rushing past and I had made no decision. At this juncture I needed to take violent action and say: 'This is right. This is what I shall do!' But then what was right? And one always hopes that the impossible will happen. So I told myself that it was not an urgent matter, and that meanwhile I must live youthfully. The last years of one's youth must not be wasted. They should be put to the best advantage.

If the weather had been warmer things might not have been so bad. But this year everybody was complaining. Even the flowers from the Scilly Isles were not coming into Covent Garden as they should. There were fewer tulips and daffodils on the London barrows, and as for the trees in Green Park they looked as if they would never burst into bud.

My problem was insoluble—or at least to resolve it I needed to be able to cut myself in two. What made it worse was that I had seen it coming for years. This painful dilemma arose out of my mother's arthritis which had now spread to every part of her body. She used to have such lovely feet and hands. Her feet were so small that she took a size smaller in shoes than I did, and her hands were white and well shaped. Her waist was so slender that when she went walking in Paris men turned to have another look. If anybody had told me that pain could reach such diabolic proportions, that it could take a foot or a hand and twist it until it looked like the gnarled bough of an apple tree, I would not have believed it. One allows for age to blow beauty softly away, but not for pain to mangle the body until even the bones are crushed. It infuriates me to think that this was the moment when, but for this devil inside her, she might have enjoyed life. Some people, neither very honest nor very good, are lucky. Things turn out well for them. Others, of whom my mother was a striking example, appear to be punished for whatever sins their forbears may have committed. As a girl my mother was lovely, but she had flaming red hair at a time when it just wasn't the fashion to be a red head. She became bitter when she was seventeen, and somehow after that whatever she did turned out wrong.

My farm in Normandy is a paradise. Mother could have it all to herself, or if she wanted company we would go and stay with her. I think she was just beginning to enjoy it when the pain began to seep through her body, attacking first one limb and then another until she could no longer sew, then no longer search for dandelion leaves in the orchard. The rest followed inexorably year by year. A summer ago it was obvious that she ought not to be left alone in the house.

But I also had a home in London and responsibilities which I had no right to abandon. If I were to become over-zealous about my mother I might lose my husband and no woman is fool enough to tempt the gods. Besides, my mother quickly tired of my presence. I got on her nerves and she had developed a passion for living alone, a trait she inherited from my grandmother at Blois who was something of a witch. When I was a child this quality endeared her to me, for children love people who are out of the ordinary.

Normally I spent every summer and early autumn with my mother on the farm, returning to London when the farmers were beating down the second crop of cider apples, the ones that keep best, from the trees. Sometimes I would stay in Normandy till All Souls' Day. I liked London in the winter, and though my flat in Shepherd Market was not very large or comfortable, it had the decided advantage of being beautifully heated.

Last summer my routine had not been quite the same. I had gone to Villers-sur-Mer in May and returned to London immediately after the French national holiday of the Fourteenth of July. My son was leaving Oxford and starting in a new job in the City and I wanted to be at hand. I went back to Villers in October for a month. Later I will tell more about this visit, as it made the most shattering impression of all upon me. People were beginning to tell me that I should either leave London altogether and take roots in Villers or put my mother in a home.

I could not leave London at this stage. It was unthinkable. But though we talked about it neither my husband nor I would ever have consented to put Matilda in a home. The alternative was to leave her alone on the farm where, if she fell or had an accident, it might be ten or twelve hours before anybody would discover her.

My eventual return to London seemed like a criminal act. I loathed myself for curling up happily in my central-heated flat and enjoying my husband's company. At night I began to have cold sweats and fantastic dreams which made me look a wreck in the morning. On top of all this I suddenly wanted to enjoy what was left of my youth. I did not wish to grow prematurely old. I practised physical jerks in front of the open window and tried to make points in ballet shoes. I wanted to drive out the devil from within me.

Didi, my Pekinese, who was now two, had become more obedient, sometimes coming when I called. Looking at him running quickly from tree to tree in the Green Park, his plumed tail held proudly on high, I recalled my complete loss of dignity when in this same park I lost him as a puppy. How badly I take things! How incapable I am of holding on to my self-control except in certain human crises in which my feminity, so helpless on lesser occasions, serves me surprisingly well! At such times my weakness can be strong. But at other times . . . Once, for instance, when learning to drive a car which I did rather late in life, I suddenly understood a manœuvre which had hitherto baffled me. My reaction was to become momentarily paralysed by joy—a sort of stroke from which I only recovered by a miracle. This surely was a sign of weakness. What woman is so stupid that she cannot learn to drive a car these days? Then to go and lose a puppy in the park!

I had found a bird—yes, it was spring again—a baby bird that had fallen from its nest. It was injured and there was a blood stain on one of its wings. I held it against my bosom wondering what to do with it. Is there any way of saving a baby bird except by putting it back in the nest? In this case the nest was nowhere to be seen, being perched, doubtless high up in the tree. The matter appeared difficult though no less poignant on that account. I must have pondered over it longer than I realized, stupidly put out by my utter incompetence and helplessness when, looking wildly about me, I suddenly realized that the puppy was no longer in view.

I searched the Green Park for what seemed hours. Wildly and with panting breath, dishevelled, an object of derision, I called the puppy by name, reverting as in all times of stress or emotion to my mother tongue. A dozen youths were playing football on the lawn by the French façade and green shutters of Lord Rothermere's house. I asked them if they had seen a Pekinese puppy. Even before they had time to answer I noticed the cruel expression that formed itself on their young features, bright with laughter a moment earlier but now forced to contemplate the ridiculous figure of a silly woman running after a lost dog. This was a moment which was to leave a scar upon me for some time to come. I have a friend who is one of the most beautiful women I have ever met. In fact I am still occasionally jealous of her because she has such poise, and seems so much at home in the various capitals of Europe where she entertains so graciously for her wealthy husband. Even she admitted having suffered this sort of dagger stab between the shoulders once when a diplomat, in describing a certain woman, turned to her and said: 'She must, like you, have been very lovely once!' Now in my mind I can still hear these youths crying out derisively: 'A peke, mate! The old girl has lost a peke!'

A policeman at the corner of Buckingham Palace, polite but indifferent, advised me to report my loss at the police station in St James's Park. What troubled me then was the thought of leaving the Green Park, because to leave it was to abandon hope of finding my dog. If, as I still believed, though not with great certainty, he was continuing his scatter-brained comings and goings between trees and among recumbent couples locked in embrace on the grass, oblivious to my distraction, happy in his freedom, running after any other dog within sight, I would not be doing myself any good by crossing the Mall and going so far away. This was an admission of defeat.

I must, however, have recovered sufficiently to be impressed by the sylvan surroundings of this charming police station. It looks like a large doll's house half hidden by shrubs and evergreens, nestling beside gardeners' huts and greenhouses belonging to Her Majesty's Office of Works, within sound of the raucous cries of the birds on the lake and the rose-throated pelicans hungry for fish. I had been directed thither by a gardener pushing a wheelbarrow, wearing a wide-brimmed felt hat turned greyish green by successive seasons of sun and showers.

'Over there!' he said.

I pushed the door open. A constable was talking on the telephone. I did not notice his rank so perhaps he was the sergeant on duty. He was bare-headed and his features were very jovial. When he laughed his wide shoulders shook in merriment. He held the telephone with one hand and with the other he painstakingly stirred the sugar in his mug of strong tea. I was suddenly angry with him, resenting the fact that he looked so happy when I was so overwrought. Finally he put the receiver down and said: 'What can I do for you?'

I gave him a detailed account of what had happened, adding that I was now exhausted and feeling thoroughly miserable. He looked at me thoughtfully and said: 'And you haven't lost it, have you?'

I fancied he was laughing at me and answered peevishly: 'I've just told you that I have!'

'I mean your accent,' he said. 'How long have you been in England?'

'That's nothing to do with my dog,' I said. 'My accent is part of me.'

'Unbelievable!' he exclaimed. 'Just like a woman! What's your name? And your address? Don't worry, Mrs Henrey, we'll find your little dog for you. I'll telephone to Scotland Yard.'

'You're going to telephone to Scotland Yard for a puppy?' I exclaimed. 'Surely they don't bother about such small things!'

I was beginning to see things in perspective. He telephoned. But then panic began to overcome me again. I was so tired that I felt like crying and this man was saying: 'You'll have to go there yourself to sign a declaration. You'll have no trouble in finding it. Make for the Cenotaph in Whitehall.'

Physically I have no endurance, or at least so I believed

until tragedy of a real kind later that spring was to teach me
that endurance is merely a matter of will-power, and that in
certain cases it lasts pretty well as long as life itself. But
when this man told me that I must now set off across Horse
Guards Parade and Whitehall to tell my story all over again
to the authorities in Scotland Yard, I felt beside myself and
wondered if I might be going to give way to hysterics. My
looks frightened me. I could do nothing to calm the wild-
ness in my eyes, and my hands were not steady enough to
remake my high-blown chignon that had lost its compact-
ness, with such a resultant loss of dignity that my entire
personality had become suspect. Somehow a touch of the
absurd always seems to creep into one's anguish. I kept on
saying to myself: 'Fancy worrying Scotland Yard about a
Pekinese. What will they say?'

Looking like a deranged woman, I arrived at the nerve
centre of so much detective fiction. I even suspect that many
of my compatriots across the Channel would have envied
me this adventure, for they are addicted to those volumes
known as the *série noire* which they indulge in like a narcotic
while buffeted by competing blasts from transistor and
television, both turned on full blast. I was requested to wait
my turn in a sort of confession box. Near by was a counter
like a bar beyond which could be seen and heard policemen
in uniform and one policewoman. My curiosity got the
better of me. I was in this box watching a play, trying to
grasp the action of the plot half way through, as in the
theatre when one arrives half an hour after the curtain has
gone up. These people were all discussing a theft which had
taken place a few hours earlier in a wealthy apartment. How
did the thief get in? What did he steal? What was his
motive? Had he a girl accomplice?

But now a curtain was to be drawn across my inquisitiveness. A police officer arrived to question me and laboriously
fill up my declaration.

'A peke?' he said thoughtfully. 'Is a peke a large dog?'

Heavens! I thought. Can one be so ignorant about pekes? 'A Chinese dog,' I said, 'very small and valuable.'

'A small dog,' he repeated. 'What colour?'

'Silver mink,' I said, 'a rather unusual colour. They're so often fiery red.'

'Let's say beige,' he said. 'Any collar?'

'Alas, no,' I answered. 'I thought he was too young to make him wear a collar. He did so hate it.'

The policeman read over what he had written and said: 'Address and telephone number, and please sign here.'

All this happened, as it seems now, a long time ago, a full two years, when a lost puppy was enough to make me feel that I had lost something irreplaceable. I recrossed Whitehall where a wreath of spring flowers was withering at the foot of the Cenotaph, and I remembered the days when men wore hats, and no man, not even a bus conductor, would pass this memorial to the blood-bath of the trenches in Flanders, and to the dead in so many other theatres of war, without uncovering himself and doubtless thinking how fortunate he was to be alive. A dozen sightseers watched the Horse Guards in their tall white boots and silver armour, motionless on black horses and stationed like living toys in front of sentry boxes. A pretty picture they made on this spring day, charmingly unreal in a world in which they no longer had any serious place. But history lay like a heat haze in layers on the other side of the street. There Charles I was beheaded; there stood the Cenotaph put up after Rupert Brooke's war, my war, and that of my battered generation; there sat on horseback two soldiers of the picture-postcard age; on those pavements would squat from time to time several thousand people, disturbed by the menace of the atom bomb and what the future might bring them.

When on my return home I opened my front door the first thing that caught my attention lying forlornly on the carpet of the hall was the doll that I had knitted for my Pekinese. That was enough to bring my tears gushing back, for I reflected that if the puppy was lost it was my fault entirely, and to my own sorrow was added the rather cowardly fear of what Robert, my husband, would have to say about it. He had bought him for me specifically to help my nerves and had claimed only a few days earlier that the peke was the only puppy he had personally taken a liking to.

When I telephoned him he said: 'You haven't a chance of getting him back. Not with the sort of crowd that goes to the Green Park on a sunny afternoon. Somebody will have stolen him. He's probably half way to Birmingham by now.'

'Why to Birmingham?' I asked.

'What a silly question,' he answered. 'I might just as well have said Liverpool or Leeds. I mean that they can dispose of him more easily in some provincial city. You know what dog thieves are!'

I was worn out. My legs were weak and I kept on telling myself that everything had been as it should have been between three and three-fifteen. I had put the wounded bird at the foot of a mighty plane tree, protecting it with some newly mown grass over which I had arranged two deck-chairs to form a roof. If nobody found it between then and closing time, if the mother bird recognized its feeble cries, there might be a chance. What made me feel sorry for myself was that in trying to do good I had lost my dog.

After dusk I went out again. I have learned to know the Green Park in many moods. When night falls it is quiet and mysterious, often deserted except for a half-sleeping figure on a bench. Piccadilly, along whose hedgerows blueberries once grew, where stagecoaches rolled between St James's Market and the west, glitters like the half-hoop of a diamond, sapphire, ruby and emerald ring. Rover, Henlys, Rover, Rootes. These words above car showrooms are spelled out in red, green and blue. The sign of the Green Park underground station in its red circle of light appears to be hovering half way between the endearing Georgian façade of the Berkeley Hotel, now painted a rather sickly sage colour, and the French early Edwardian stone of the Ritz, with the great windows of its dining-room banked with hydrangeas. The In and Out Club opposite what were once the wrought-iron gates of Devonshire House is having a party, and as in Victorian nights when mem-sahibs were somebodies, gas flares burn outside, giving the club a fine air. The windows are lit up. You may see gentlemen in evening dress escorting their wives and daughters all dressed up for the occasion. Music wafts across Piccadilly, while in the rockery to the right of the ceremonial entrance to the club a duck and a drake have made their nest. When their young are old enough to walk they will lead them unafraid across Piccadilly to take the air in the park.

The wide avenue of tall plane trees leads from the never opened Devonshire House gates to the Victoria Memorial opposite Buckingham Palace. The Queen is in residence and the Royal Standard, floodlit against the purple night, gives another glimpse of the grandeur of an age that is slipping past. An air liner wheels high above, doubtless waiting for the signal to land at London Airport. More of them drone overhead, bound for whatever part of the globe your imagination chooses—Nairobi or Cape Town, Delhi or San Francisco. Here are the homes of millionaires whose windows all face the nocturnal quietness of the Green Park and look out over the lawns and trees to Buckingham Palace and the traffic flowing along Piccadilly and Constitution Hill to the great road works beyond. To the west a floodlit crane stands at the very summit of what soon was to be London's tallest and newest hotel.

I call and call, but there is no point in calling. I haven't even the heart to go and see whether my wounded bird is still beneath its makeshift roof of deck-chairs.

I had not been home very long when the telephone rang. My Pekinese was at Vine Street police station. My husband went to collect him in a cab.

'He is very dirty,' he said. 'You had better give him a bath.'

While I was drying him he snapped and bit me savagely on the nose so that it bled. Either he had forgotten me or he was having his revenge.

For several days he gave no sign of being my dog. He sulked in corners. But it had not been so very long since he had been torn from his mother, sold like Joseph to strangers, lost in a park and taken to prison. He had a right to feel aggrieved.

To own a dog in London is madness. There is no staying in bed in the morning. He expects me to do the whole round of Green Park before 8 a.m. and to be back there a full half-hour before it closes. On the whole I prefer the morning walk, for it is then that the Green Park is most countrified. The lawns are so fresh and damp underfoot that it is wise to wear bootees. The air is still pure and sweet. Men carrying prongs arrive to pick up any stray pieces of paper that may still be lying about, and these they drop into a wicker basket, rather like a lobster basket, slung over their backs. The lamplighter comes along on his bicycle to put out the gaslight in the old-fashioned park standards; he leans his bicycle against a tree, does what is necessary and rides off again balancing his tall stave across his shoulder like a trick rider in a circus. There is a supervisor from a telephone exchange who lives in one of the small white houses in Shepherd Market, and who likes to exercise her poodles in the park before she reports for the early shift.

Apart from these *habitués*, few are those one meets at this time of day along these tree-lined avenues, these gravel paths, on these well-kept lawns, and it requires but little imagination to tell oneself that, like a great lady of the past, one has an estate of one's own in the centre of the town.

Soon after eight o'clock the first crowds of office workers begin to stream across the Green Park from Victoria station. Sometimes I envy the career girl; at other times I am glad to bring my little dog home and to enjoy the sensation of freedom that idleness gives me. I can dawdle over breakfast, knit small squares of coloured wool to make a bedspread of many colours, or dream. A woman is fortunate indeed when she has a husband who does not oblige her to go to work or, to be more precise, one who earns enough to make it unnecessary for her to supplement his income. Yet what do we mean by 'work'?

For most of us the best time of our lives is not at the office, as shorthand typist or private secretary, choosing a dress with the money in our pay envelope and gossiping with the other girls, but at home bringing up a child. The rub is what happens afterwards, how to prevent our brains from losing their initial sharpness. For like machinery, the mind gets rusty after only a few months. The hiatus of childbirth proves both our joy and our intellectual undoing. The Chinese Communists claim that this is a waste of potential brainpower. The girl should receive an education equal to that of the boy; she should compete professionally against him both before she has had her children and afterwards. Presumably *ad infinitum*. But even if this were possible, would so much additional brainpower make the world a pleasanter place to live in? A surfeit of efficiency might eventually embarrass us like too many motor-cars, and I doubt if women want to compete professionally all through their lives against men.

These problems quickly become boring. When an educated

girl is young, office work can be very pleasant. No girl in her senses would willingly miss it, any more than she would want to throw away the chance of higher education if she were clever enough to get a place at Oxford or Cambridge. The gossip of young career women is often nowadays that of serious people who have their own apartments, their independence, their carefully balanced views on politics and literature. They earn as much as men, and use the office telephone to converse on psychological problems with their friends of both sexes.

The trouble is that the career girl, like the private secretary, can no longer afford to grow old. Her charm is in her youth. She can be clever but she must be young. She may possibly go back to work after having had one child, but she is not likely to do so after the second or the third. Whereas the man, like a good wine, matures with age.

So when I see these crowds of office workers streaming from Victoria across the Green Park, I reflect that I am indeed fortunate to enjoy the luxury of idleness. I can spend as long as I like thinking about trivial matters. This is one immense advantage we have over men, who are always either too busy or too tired to ponder illogically about the surprising things that surround us. For, as Théophile Gautier pointed out, it is the unessential that matters. What is useful or necessary is apt to be a bore. A touch of vagary helps to compensate for so much that is lustreless in life.

When first she came to England, my mother was often critical of the partiality that Englishwomen of the period showed for large beflowered hats, brightly coloured dresses and glass beads. The female population of the island had a reputation amongst the Latin races for wanting to copy the bright colours of the parrot. Experience has taught me to view with indulgence the desire of older women to hide the loss of their beauty with beads and rainbow colours. If on occasion they present a painful spectacle it is that the mind revolts before the shortness of youth. Why do we have to look like thirty when we still dream like twenty, especially when we realize that owing to *gaucherie* or shyness we missed so many of those early opportunities?

At a store in the West End I am powerfully drawn to the remnants counter where there are undulating waves of pure silk and splashes of rich brocade. I hear the babble of foreign tongues which leads me to suppose that some of these visitors from abroad find here the attraction and colour of the proverbial oriental quarter with its sharp prismatic brilliance. The saris of the Indian women make their skin glow in the artificial light.

I bought a length of white worsted with which to make a tight skirt to wear with a thigh-length pullover. When I examined it more carefully at home I found a stain which I tried to remove with benzine. A wide circle of unpalatable grey was the only result. I accordingly plunged the entire piece into a bath of warm water and detergent, but on ironing it I saw immediately that my acquisition had lost that freshness which had made it so desirable in my eyes and which alone had been the reason for my buying it. Suddenly I no longer wanted to turn it into a smart tight-fitting skirt. I was disgusted with it, and looking out into the courtyard I saw that rain was falling. An announcer on the radio, in a voice that seemed to take a perverse pleasure in slowly emitting bad news, prophesied a spell of wet weather. Emptying a wicker basket full of hoarded remnants on to the bed, I decided to cut myself a blouse out of some chiffon bought the previous year. Disdaining a pattern, I cut boldly into the light, slippery material, ran up the seams on the machine and tried it on in front of the mirror. I told myself that it was pretty, a little on the sombre side but elegant. My Pekinese concluded that this change of attire signified an excursion into the Green Park, and he sought, by looking appealingly into my eyes, to encourage my good intention.

As by now the rain had stopped and the sun was shining again, I was glad to put the blouse aside and escape from the monotony of the house. So I put on the thigh-length pull-over in honour of which I had bought the ill-fated remnant of white worsted.

My dog and I had no sooner arrived in the Green Park than we met the lady Pekinese, Bamboo, and her pretty and delightful mistress. We walked unhurriedly under the dripping boughs of the plane trees while Bamboo's owner reminisced.

An air liner passing rather low in that direction they always seemed to take, coming from the north-east, break-ing into view from under a cloud half way between the Berkeley and the Ritz, it flashed reflected sunshine from out of a patch of blue sky that seemed to belie the promise of more rain and then sped off south-west, losing itself again in more clouds over the gardens of Buckingham Palace. Bamboo's owner had paused in what she was saying to watch its progress. Now, as if in imagination she had travelled this short distance in the air liner about which we knew nothing, not even its nationality, she said:

'I was once an air hostess on Comets. This is the age of romance for the ambitious, high-spirited girl. I floated through a dreamlike evocation of the *Arabian Nights*, and it was even more fabulous than being a mannequin in a top Paris fashion house or being an international cover girl. I had first wanted to be an actress, and in fact made a long apprenticeship in repertory, but I came up against the usual difficulties of finding a job in a West End show, and in a fit of peevishness joined the flying personnel of an air line.

'My life became a fairy story. I bought silk in the markets of India and South Africa which I had made up into dresses in Hong Kong and Colombo, and on every journey I went to collect the clothes I had ordered on the preceding trip. For a young woman what can surpass the thrill of having her dresses and suits made specially for her by deft fingers working in the four corners of the globe to enhance her beauty?

'We were delayed in Cairo once while an engine was being repaired. As the passengers were in a hurry the company sent out another Comet from England. The pilot of this relief plane was destined to become my husband. Thus love touched me gently on the shoulder under the burning skies of Egypt. Neither he nor I fly any more, though occasionally we are overcome by nostalgia.'

While she spoke our two Chinese dogs chased each other with a sort of oriental dignity from tree to tree.

'So much flying has spoilt me for train journeys,' Bamboo's owner went on. 'At one time my parents lived at Hove and the journey seemed endless. Now my father is dead and my mother lives at Wimbledon, but even that seems far away.'

Whenever the weather made it possible I spent these early spring afternoons with my dog in the park as I had done with a previous Pekinese during the war. The Green Park *habitués* were very different now. A group of coloured girls wearing bright cotton dresses and men's felt hats arrive every afternoon and sit on the grass in a circle. They talk and sometimes they sing. Didi, my dog, pays them a visit and I see their long ebony-coloured fingers moving through his silver mink fur.

My dog comes back to steal some bread I throw to the birds. He sniffs the warm loaf in my basket, for I buy it from the baker on my way to the park, knowing that this is the hour he brings it hot out of the oven. Didi, where bread is concerned, has the same instincts as had my son when he was a baby. He liked to smell its warm goodness and steal a piece of the crust.

Mrs James de Rothschild arrives from time to time with her Pekinese. Another is led on a leash by a servant and,

like a rich child, looks enviously at Didi and Bamboo who
can do what they please. If I had a fairy godmother who
asked me what I would like I would choose of course one
of those wide, terraced apartments that overlook these
beautiful lawns. It must be heavenly to wake up in the
morning and walk through wide french windows and have
breakfast on a balcony hung with plants and sweet with the
upwafted scent of May. My desires change from year to
year. I want to be beyond the reach of Diesel fumes, as high
up as Semiramis, Queen of Babylon, in her hanging gardens,
and yet I want a full view of the wonders of the modern
town.

From time to time I think of the sands of Villers-sur-Mer,
and of Patsy with her new baby Philip, who necessitated her
fourth Caesarian. She went to a nursing home one September afternoon straight from a cocktail party she had given
specially for her friends, and three days later she returned to
Montauzan with the baby. Jacques, her husband, put in oil-
fired central heating and had the house repainted. Patsy
bought the newest two-horse-power Citroën. It was yellow
that year. The makers change the colour of each new model
so that the year of manufacture can instantly be recognized.
She also replenished her wardrobe, having of necessity
bought no clothes during the summer of her pregnancy.

Bamboo's owner left me sitting by the bandstand where
bands no longer play, such Edwardian distractions being
replaced by the ubiquitous and insolent transistor. In the
room underneath, where scarlet-coated musicians used to
rest and smoke a cigarette during the interval, gardener-
scavengers now store the steel prongs they use to pick up
litter from the lawns. Their baskets line the walls. There was
a time when this corner of the Green Park, with a band
playing rousing marches or musical comedy tunes, evoked
fashionable continental spas: Baden-Baden, perhaps, or
Wildbad in the Black Forest. Now the bandstand has

become a sort of gazebo with London glittering all around, famous landmarks encircling my contentment.

During the October I spent with my mother in France she had spoken of her birthday in a way unlike her usual manner, and now her words came back to me. She seldom mentioned such events, disliking anything that in the slightest manner could lead to family exuberance or sentiment. Her own birthday fell in the first week of December and apropos of this she had said: 'At my age every additional year is buckshee—an unexpected present.' This was in conflict with her frequent outbursts about wishing she were dead. She was too intelligent not to rise in revolt against the rapid deterioration of her physical powers. When she was not being driven half mad by pain, her mind, which was keen and critical—too critical —took such a violent dislike to herself that she longed for annihilation. It gave her a sort of perverse satisfaction to see the panic on my face not only at the thought of losing her but also at hearing her proclaim almost fiendishly that oblivion was a cheap price to pay to be rid of the wreckage of her body and to be released from pain.

Faced by this bleak prospect, for it was as bleak for me as it was for her, I enjoyed all the more the pleasures of London. I found myself saying: 'Every additional day spent in London free with my little dog is buckshee, an unexpected present!' My desire to make the best of them plunged me into a frenzy of harmless nothings. I chose wool to make a new pullover. As soon as I started to knit it I prayed that I should have time to finish it. I translated a page of Greek. I experimented with a new hair-do. I indulged in an orgy of film-going. I was fortunate in being invited to the private showings of all the new films and I seldom missed one. My husband was fiction editor of a mass circulation women's magazine, and films for serialization came under the general umbrella of his interests. I always made a point of sharing his more pleasurable duties. He worked with a staff of young and extremely intelligent women, and strove in concert with them to find material acceptable to several million women readers. This sort of work was closely enough allied to my own to make it fun. Even the office small talk enthralled me, and I often wondered why one of the girls—they were all gifted—did not write a novel of London life, as so many career girls in New York have done, to recount her adventures. Their ambitions, love stories and quarrels provided me with just that antidote I needed to counter the drama that was being enacted in Normandy. I worried about those from out of town who complained that it took time to meet the right sort of boys in London. I loved it when one of them telephoned me or when at film sessions they confided in me. The very films were a source of excitement. A form of escapism from my constant misery. Every time the lights went out and the title was flashed on the screen and the names of the actors and actresses set out, I experienced that delicious moment of hope, of enchanting promise that is the very texture of life itself. When a new day breaks who can tell its outcome? When a young girl looks ahead with all her life to spend—a girl who has not yet broken into her hoard—this, she would say to herself, is the beginning.

How quickly the days went by. I was ashamed of them. And yet how long it seemed between my mother's letters, for every time she wrote saying that she was not worse I had a reprieve. Even if she was a little worse, but not driven helpless to her bed, then at least the letter was not so much a cry for help that I must go at once. I might stay in London a few more days. I tried to read into them more hope than they contained. If only the warm weather would come, I thought. This prolonged cold is her enemy—and mine. I had implored her to write once a week but it did not depend only on herself. She had to write the letters, but must rely on

other people to post them when it suited them to go down
to the village. I think she usually wrote on Fridays, sitting at
the kitchen table with a school pen and a pot of French ink.
French ink never looks the same as English ink. The
colours are different. Every word was torture, and although
the writing had begun to have a rather spidery effect, she
had an amazing sense of literary style and of the dramatic.
She invariably picked up the high lights of village gossip,
even though she no longer went there, and always put
drama into the adventures of her hens and her cats. Fifille,
the female Pekinese I had taken over from London, had
adopted my mother as soon as I left the farm. But loved
though Fifille was, she never came as close to my mother's
heart as did her cats. My mother's love for her cats was part
of the witch complex. She would spend hours brewing
things for them on the Aga stove, murmuring to herself or
to them as she did so, and the house would be filled with the
smell of that special cooking which so excited the animals.
They arched their backs, put up their tails and rubbed
themselves against her poor deformed legs. When I wasn't
there I fancy they all talked to one another incessantly.

I had, of course, been to see her since October, but the
October visit was the one I thought about most. Apple-
picking time is my favourite season of the year; and then
also it had been harder to leave her with winter coming on
than it had been when I went over again for a few days in
January after a business trip to Paris. I saw her again in
March when I could hope that spring was already on its
way.

I said that I would describe in detail the events of the
October journey if only to rid myself of their haunting
memory. I sometimes think I would have done better to
stay with her the whole winter rather than to come back to
London seeking forgetfulness and only finding this miserable tearing at my conscience. The truth is that one can

never run away from one's duty, if indeed I can be certain that this was or ought to have been my duty. I cannot prove it either way to my own satisfaction.

Even before this visit I was already haunted by the thought of a single drug—cortisone. Cortisone was both her joy and her relief and her most cruel and determined enemy. The relief she gained from it was stupendous; the harm it did her was shattering. At times I saw it as something heaven-sent while at other times I saw it as a killer: a killer without a face, a hooded killer with a dagger poised over my mother's heart. But she cried out for this murderer, and then I capitulated, for pity itself demanded it. In point of fact I had little say in the matter since she had no difficulty in obtaining as much as she wanted, and I think that if she had she would almost have murdered to get it. Here again my conscience was brought into the dance, for she believed, and I think accurately, that cortisone was the only drug which could prevent her from being nailed to her bed—and that for my mother would have meant the end, the final disgrace, the capitulation, the asking to be taken away to a home. So had I right to interfere, to say to her: 'I am going to rob you of your chance to move about at will in this house which as long as you live is your domain. I am going to nail you to your bed'? No, I had not that right, for life without freedom is not worth anything. But all the same when I told my friends about the quantities of cortisone my mother imbibed every day they looked at me aghast, exclaiming: 'She will lose the power of speech. Her intestines will be burnt up. She will go blind. You are killing her.' Then the nightmare would flare up.

Except in the height of summer when there is an air service direct to Deauville, which allows me to travel between London and my farm in just over an hour, the journey is long and tiring. One travels on the night boat from Southampton to Le Havre, and then there are nearly three hours in a bus which, in spite of its petrol engine, retains much of the character of a stagecoach in the days of Flaubert and Maupassant. The peasantry is still very important in this province.

I remember every detail of this journey. I recall, for instance, that the ship's purser who had looked after me since my first voyage after the Liberation of France was doing his last trip before he was being made to retire, and that my stewardess was not the one I usually had. The other, poor soul, had died from smoking too many cigarettes. The news of her death and the idea of what she must have suffered if, as I supposed, she died of cancer of the lung, tainted my journey with melancholy from its very beginning. I would have needed to be stronger minded than I am not to have started drawing comparisons between this woman's craving for nicotine and my mother's craving for cortisone. The impression that this news made on me is enough to show in what state of nerves I must have been.

Yet how pleased I was at six in the morning to find the coach waiting for us and to start rolling across the Norman countryside, listening to André, the driver, exchanging news with his passengers. Now that the Tancarville bridge spans the great width of the Seine we no longer need to cross in the car ferry. I was almost sorry about this. In the past very often I met on this ferry the old woman who dealt in holly and mistletoe at Christmas time. She once confided in me that she had fourteen children—'Some of 'em dead and some of 'em alive, some of 'em good and some of 'em bad.' Last autumn the son with whom she had elected to live, while cleaning out his shot gun to go after rabbits and hares on the first of September for *l'ouverture de la chasse*, had shot himself dead through the heart. For the time being she was staying on with her daughter-in-law, but if the daughter-in-law remarried she would go and live with another son in the colonies. She had no idea in which colony he lived, for when she wrote to him she merely copied the address from the back of the envelope, and then she forgot it until he wrote again. In the spring she dealt in lilac. I recall her saying to me one lovely April day: 'As you see me at this moment, I am off to pick lilac in the garden of a very rich man who lives near Le Havre. He allows me to pick as much as I can carry, and I sell it on Sundays outside church in the morning and outside the cemetery after lunch. This year will be the last year because he's going to sell his house and retire to a home for the aged. In spite of his wealth he is so old that he has no friends left, and so he thinks that he'll be less lonely in a home. He said he was sorry about the lilac, but I said to him: "There's nothing to worry about because by next year the ferry will be closed" —owing to the new bridge, you understand—"so that I couldn't get across the water to pick your lilac."'

'But there will be the bridge,' I objected.

The old woman looked disdainful. 'The bridge will not be the same,' she said, 'and the bridge will be at Tancarville, not here. Besides, I'm getting old.' She repeated with tears in her eyes as she laughed: 'I'm getting old and soon I'll not be picking dandelion leaves and daffodils and lilac, or even holly and mistletoe, on the other side of the water. It will all be finished. Finished it will be. Ain't I right, Monsieur André?'

The bus driver nodded his head sympathetically. 'Everything comes to an end,' he said.

There is a good ten miles from Le Havre to the engineering marvel which is the new bridge at Tancarville. After crossing it, being suspended high above the swirling water and feeling a little seasick as one sways gently in the bus, one travels back on the other bank to the mouth of the Seine, where the woods and rich orchards run down to the water, which is half fresh water, half salt water. Great ships move up and down the estuary between the sea and Rouen. We thus travel the best part of twenty miles to come back opposite to the place from which we started. My old lady of the lilac was right to regret the ferry, because the ferry brought us across nearer to the mouth, and it was more picturesque, though it was unreliable when a sea mist hid the banks. All along the road school children stop Monsieur André on this early morning run. They are off to school at Honfleur. After passing Honfleur other children from the school at Trouville stop the bus, and if there are no seats they merely crowd round Monsieur André in a way which would never be allowed in an English bus, and the little girls all practise their charms on him, which of course is very French. They have nicknamed him the Admiral because of the gold braid on his cap. Monsieur André never wears his cap except when driving through a large bourg or a town, and then he puts it on because he is afraid that if he is seen by an inspector from the bus company while in what the French call 'agglomerations' it might be thought undignified for a bus driver to be bare-headed. The little girls titter at Monsieur André and show off their busts which already give them an air of being little women. Monsieur André, like King David, warms his older bones at this contact with youthful feminity. He also shows off a bit, charming the little girls by his witty sallies, careful, however, to utter no word that might shock his charming audience. Thus the journey never fails to bring me softly back into the atmosphere of apple orchards and half-timbered houses, of market-places, slate roofs, thatched roofs and vistas of golden sand. At Villers-sur-Mer I leave my travelling companions and collect my small Citroën from the garage. I drive up the steep main road for half a mile, turn into a quiet lane and am soon looking down into the valley where the slate roof of my own half-timbered house shimmers in the sun.

As soon as I drive into my own orchard, leaving the car

by the white railings which surround my garden, Fifille, my Pekinese, comes out barking joyfully and the cats arch their backs against my legs. The kitchen door is always open. I hurried to it this October morning, and there at the end of the white deal table sat my mother, as she always sat, still golden haired and wearing her apron and waiting like a good little girl.

I kissed her—not too effusively, for she disliked any pronounced show of affection. Now in my joy at returning home I did not feel anything like enough gratitude for this miracle which allowed me to find her sitting in the centre of my house like a presiding angel, giving it the warmth and love of her presence. For the moment I took that presence for granted and, slamming down my suitcases and hold-alls on the tiled floor, I ran back into the front garden to enthuse over the roses which nobody picked any more and to look wonderingly over the garden railings at the apple trees without number. Hundreds of apple trees there were, heavy with golden fruit. They stretched all the way down to the stream and all the way up on the other side as far as the road to St Vaast and beyond that again to the Louis XIII château which far away in the distance peeps out from between its double curtain of trees.

This sight then, as it always does, made me breathless.

I ran back into the house, and the house, as it were, went to my head. How did I ever believe that I could live without it? How could I ever imagine it without the warmth of the Aga stove in the kitchen and the presence of my mother at the corner of the table, nursing her bad eye with her poor hand whose knuckles stood out like walnuts.

I went to the back of the house. On the patio the hens scattered at my coming, forgetting that I had played with most of them on the kitchen table when they were chicks. One or two rejected by a mother hen had been raised to sturdiness by being put on a piece of blanket over the stove.

The kitchen garden had a wild look about it. Weeds grew in the paths. Matilda could do no more gardening.

I fell again quickly into the pattern of country life. But before I speak of that I must touch on the difficult part of my stay, for unless I can explain it exactly the whole picture will be out of focus. The house, hidden amongst its farms and orchards, was mine. Though at times I felt we had done the wrong thing by coming here while most of our interests were in London, and while I still dreamed of a cottage in England, my attachment for this tiny domain was probably greater than I realized. But every time I came here it was at the cost of leaving my husband in London. The journey was too difficult and expensive for him to join me often. There was, for example, no service by Le Havre on Sunday nights, so that week-end visits were impracticable. He also thought it wise to push forward with our affairs in London while I prepared Villers against the day when we could make it our chief home. But we never envisaged the place without my mother. She was here when my son was born, and kept it in safety for us when we both had to be away. Our debt, quite apart from our love, was incalculable. But there were moments during these brief stays when her continual presence in the kitchen—her way of watching and passing judgment, or at least so I fancied—gave me the impression that I was not mistress in my own home. This streak of bitterness in me might have been easier to eradicate if my husband had been more often there, though the presence of an aged parent—especially that of a mother who intimidates her daughter to the point of panic—can sadly upset the difficult balance between wife and husband.

That first October evening, while the farmers were picking apples in the orchard, Matilda gave me a résumé of small happenings. These quickly degenerated into complaints. A tap leaked. Did I realize there was no more coke for the Aga? And why had I brought her no Horlicks?

Didn't I know that this was what she wanted most? 'You should have told me,' I said. 'Just a word in a letter. But I have brought you some of those English sausages you like so much.'

'You could have saved yourself the trouble,' she said. 'I don't like them any more.'

All the shopping I had done in Shepherd Market with such joy in my heart now turned sour on me. I went off to tidy up the house. The cats (there were far too many of them) had soiled the carpets. I must tread softly and learn for a month not to sing or to laugh, to repress every sign of happiness for fear that it might be construed as a lack of sympathy. Pain and bitterness were twin masters in the house. I must share the grudges and antagonisms of old age and yet expect to be treated like a girl of ten. 'Why didn't you guess there was no Horlicks?' 'Can't you keep quiet, instead of making all that noise!'

I went to bed early and put on the radio. My bedroom is the most beautiful room in the house, with its books and cupboards and the little private bathroom designed by myself. The country air was unbelievably good, and in the morning I awoke to the autumnal glory of birds and flowers. During the war I had a dear Pekinese called Pouffy. He used to ride on the coverlet of my baby's pram when I walked in the Green Park. He died in Normandy and I planted a rose tree on his grave. Now his rose tree was full of magnificent blooms. How angrily he used to bark when the bombs fell on Piccadilly! How brave he was during the period of the flying bombs! I brought him here on our first return to France. He was the best loved of all my Pekinese. He would sit contentedly under my chair, never leave me an instant, refuse to eat when I was not with him. When at last I had him put to sleep, I took a rose tree from the front garden where it had never seemed happy and planted it on his grave. As in some story in the

Arabian Nights the rose tree suddenly started giving an abundance of beautiful red roses. It had become the pride of my garden.

Fifille replaced Pouffy, and now it struck me that she also was growing old, or perhaps it was merely by comparison with Didi, who was so young and playful. It needed all the beauty of the farm in the rich colourings of a fine October and the lonely majesty of those glorious golden sands to compensate for the panic which overwhelmed me at times. I was alone in the house with the bitter recriminations of my mother as my only diversion. She was suffering now beyond her capacity to endure it cheerfully. At meal times she would bring her head down into her plate and eat like an animal. I think I would have taken it better at seventeen than now when I was haunted by the fear of suddenly breaking the barrier between what I was and what so quickly I could become. Pain and bitterness do not necessarily go together. There are shining exceptions to every rule. But my mother in her long life of disappointment and despair, of early poverty and frustration, had taken just about as much as any woman can take. Until long past her widowhood she had never had a penny of her own, she had been robbed of the only jewel in her crown, her baby son, and in order to give me the necessities of life she had been obliged to bend over her lace making blouses until long after my father had collapsed exhausted on the bed. Even the Second World War had not spared her. Had we not left her alone and miserable on the quay at St Malo while with my baby in arms we sailed safely away to England? There were memories that scalded me. After the horrors of the German occupation my mother had gone back alone to this pillaged farmhouse to become the prey of people bent on her destruction. In all the great crises of her life she had never had a shoulder to lean on, a voice to advise her, a friend to whom she could turn. Ill fortune did more than shadow her.

It sought her out. It waited at street corners for her, and then took her savagely by the throat.

Yes, she moaned. She sat for hours at one end of the kitchen table, her hand across her bad eye, and maybe at times she even took evil pleasure in hurting the person who loved her best. And in me bubbled and boiled a desire not to be tied indefinitely to a spirit of bitterness and discontent. Give me the wind and the rain! Give me the long white road and the excitement of tomorrow! Give me just a few more years of inquisitiveness and achievement! Oh, how passionately I want to live!

In the kitchen garden there were leeks and French beans and ripening tomatoes, and a glorious, untidy bed of late sweet peas. The cows on the other side of the hedge came to watch me working in the strawberry patch, hoping that I would begin to dig and throw them tempting morsels of green leaf and vegetable. The weather remained constantly fine. I never tire of saying that autumn is my favourite season! The bees droned and the birds sang and I picked baskets of ripe pears.

Then a sort of miracle happened. Matilda had inherited from her mother the secret of jam making. I have never in my life tasted anything to equal the jam that my grandmother made at Blois from the fruit of her walled garden on the banks of the Loire. But then of course she was a witch and cast a spell over it. Matilda also could cast a spell. She took the pears I brought in that October and made just two or three pots of jam. I find the word jam inadequate to describe the sort of whole *glacé* fruit, which when cold crystallized in the pots and seemed when one ate it to have retained the droning of the bees and the hot sun. This was Matilda's peculiar cry of independence, her way of saying: 'You see that I am still up and active! I don't need anybody's help!' We stored and graded the eating apples, and brought in the walnuts from the great tree behind the house. We were like busy ants storing winter provisions.

This month of October has suddenly become so important to me that for the first time in my life I distrust my memory. Fortunately there are still my letters, those long letters which then as always flowed from my pen. For when unable to sleep I write to my husband in the quiet hours of the night. It was my mother-in-law, herself a superb letter writer, who first made me aware that I had this natural gift for setting down the events of the day. But I have always considered writing letters to those I love as a means of putting my mind at rest before courting sleep last thing at night and I have never tried to give them form or the slightest literary merit. Few are dated and I am only now gradually curing myself of this defect, but if I look through the October letters, quoting passages here and there, I want to make it clear that my object in so doing is to reassure myself that the picture I have tried to paint of the period is not coloured by later events. For what is truth? There are so many facets of the same thing.

'MY LOVE,

'I write to you because this is the week-end, and once again we are separated from each other. The weather yesterday was superb, sunshine and Indian summer heat. As it was Thursday the farmers and their children were in all the surrounding orchards picking apples. So of course were ours; and at half past four Jacques Déliquaire, Georgette, his pretty wife, and Brigitte, their adorable little girl, not forgetting the Polish granny, broke off work to have a meal of cheese and cider on a white cloth at the foot of an apple tree. Nothing has changed in this enchanting country since Manet painted "Le Déjeuner sur l'Herbe". Since in the middle of this Norman atmosphere I occasionally revert to English customs, I served tea for David's benefit in the kitchen. He had come to help me cut the grass and prune the rose trees. The Zeiss binoculars you bought me at Harrods for my birthday are proving a joy to my mother, who takes them with her when we drive down to the sands. She can, without leaving the car, sweep the distant horizon like a British admiral. When the trees are bare I shall be able, by looking out of my bedroom window, to see what is happening in all the most distant orchards. I called on Patsy Poirot. Her baby boy can already walk a little and he is a treasure, as friendly as he is a picture of health. Patsy has taken to playing golf with Mado Duprez, Annette and Michel Laurent are on a business trip to New York. I fancy their trip is making some of the others a bit jealous. Annette in a letter to Patsy told her that she had seen Paris models at Macy's with the original *griffe* for twenty-five pounds, and there was mink on everything: mink on the collars and mink on the cuffs, stoles of mink and mink coats. Will she come back covered in mink? That is the question that all our young women are asking in this fascinating coterie, whose members are real one hundred per cent feminine women, happy that their husbands should buy mink for them rather than want to turn them into career girls. I must get you the name of the United States laboratory for which Michel is working. I hear good reports about it, and it may be quoted on the New York Stock Exchange. I slept badly last night, which of course is nothing new, except that there was a different reason for it. Some beast was trying to get out through the window which overlooks the château, the one I keep closed at night, and I couldn't make the silly creature understand that the other one was as always wide open. Was it an owl or a bat? I went to fetch a broom and finally fell asleep still grasping it. When I woke up the sun was shining and all the male dogs from the neighbouring farms were waiting for Fifille, who has entered her interesting period. It amused me to wonder what would happen if

Didi were here. Now that the season is over the people in our village are all taking their holidays. Mme Baudon has gone off on a cruise to Greece, the woman who keeps the haberdasher's shop is away and the creamery is closed. The *garde champêtre* who has the young wife who became paralysed a year ago sent for a healer, who placed his hands against hers and the young woman, so the story goes, immediately rose from out of her numbness and walked, with the result that a neighbour who suffers from asthma was so impressed that he wants to send for the healer. This is all on the authority of the good Mme Javault. I shall take mother down to market in the car before lunch. The new hot-water system is miraculous and Granny says it saved her life when I was away. Washing up has become a pleasure. While I have been writing these few lines a slight mist has come up from the sea, putting a veil across the sun. According to the traditions of my family I have become a witch by day, pulling up weeds and nettles, but in the evening I am transformed into another Penelope, undoing pullovers that are too small and reknitting them. Mado, doubtless to emulate the ladies of Macy's, has a mink stole (this from Patsy). Please go to Gamba and get me some dancing shoes, size four.

'*Saturday*. The mist on Friday the 13th lasted well until lunch time, but though the market was seen but dimly, the produce was all that one expects in this fabulously rich province. My farmer's wife from Branville, the one I like to patronize on these occasions, sold me a kilo of butter of her own making which we were glad to bring back. After lunch I decided to autumn-clean my bedroom. You may recall that I put a piece of oak in the stone fireplace to turn it into a bookshelf. I was surprised to find traces of a sticky substance which at first I could not recognize. I dipped a finger rather gingerly into it, tasted it and discovered that it was honey. Just think of it. Bees must have swarmed here in my absence. I interpret this as a good omen, for like Napoleon I love them. But where did they go after so thoughtfully leaving me this present? I must investigate. I had a better night, and as I had put some bread into the hanging coconut I was awakened by the birds.

'*Monday.* I spent Sunday tidying up everywhere—the house, the garden, the farmyard. Georgette arrived this morning to ask Granny to telephone to Dozulé. I was surprised how well she did it, asking the vet in her little girl's voice to come urgently for a cow who is expecting to have her calf this evening. (Later.) The cow gave birth to a magnificent heifer. The vet arrived on time and everything went splendidly. By coincidence one of our neighbours had the same excitement on his farm. While I am on the subject of farms and farmers I must tell you that people are talking about a certain bull over Blonville way who is accused of having given gonorrhoea to the cows which were taken to him. His owner claims that he has been cured, but I gather that this will not prevent him from being destroyed. Jacques Déliquaire has bought his family a television set. This may not impress you as much as it does us. Everybody in England has television, but on our Norman farms it is still a very new toy to be discussed and wondered at. So you can picture our farmers, Jacques and Georgette and Brigitte, in their dear little farmhouse, all going to bed early to watch television, for they have put the set in their bedroom. I must now think seriously about buying one for Granny. I would like to have it put in before I leave her for the winter. I gave David Owen the *Everyman's Encyclopaedia of Gardening* which you sent out for his birthday. As for me I am for the second time in my life deep in Mme de Staël's masterpiece *Corinne.* It needed my journey to Rome last year to appreciate certain parts. For the moment it is casting a spell over me, and I can think of nothing else. This also is what I find in it. You can imagine the effect it has made on me.

They will disappear, have no doubt about it, those parents who are taking so long to make way for you . . . that mother whose old age imposes duties on you that you find inconvenient; they will disappear, those careful watchers over your childhood, those lively protectors of your adolescence; they will disappear and you will search in vain for better friends; they will disappear, and as soon as they are no longer here, they will strike you in a new light because time, which makes older those who are alive, who are in view of us, makes them seem younger as soon as death has taken them away.

'I have been drawing up accounts to see how much it costs me to run the house, and I don't think I can do it much under ten pounds a week. Of course that takes care of everything: drugs, coal, grain for the farmyard, light, an occasional charwoman and food. The birds are a great pleasure, and I have bought three carnations to plant in the front garden.

'*Wednesday*. I write to you on a sheet of notepaper I must have stolen from the Mayfair Hotel that evening we went to that fabulous party with your young colleague Muriel-Jane Smith. Do you remember the millionaire's suite? Yesterday I emptied and cleaned one of the big water tanks in the garden, the one under my bedroom window, and I watered every single rose tree. Jacques Déliquaire's cows are still in the home field, and his little daughter Brigitte, who is my very good friend, comes to play cards with us while her parents are milking. I take Granny out in the car every afternoon and we criss-cross the Pays d'Auge, choosing the deserted lanes which she likes best. A man came to offer me three hundred pounds for eighty trees in the big wood, amongst which are fifteen oaks, two beech trees and thirty-four ash. I indignantly said no. I feel sure you will agree. I spent part of the afternoon at Montauzan, which is beautifully heated, whereas here, except for the kitchen, it reminds me of a small cold cage. The fact is that I'm too lazy to put on the heating and so I go to bed at eight o'clock—even earlier sometimes—and transact all my business in bed with Fifille and the cats on the eiderdown.

'*Thursday*. I've been planting cabbages, spreading manure over the kitchen garden and trying to saw some logs, but the effort was too much for me, and when I switched on the electric saw the belt slipped and so I gave up in disgust. I'm beginning to envy the Archers who, on the B.B.C., seem to have as many men as they can use about the farm! At the farm on the other side of the stream, Rémi's wife is daily expecting her baby. Rémi's parents, who are not, as you know, at all from this part of the world, have decided to come and live near their son and daughter-in-law, and have found a house next to Mme Javault's along the road to St Vaast. Rémi père and his wife are both still young, and are even bringing two other children with them, one aged sixteen and another fourteen. So here is a family that, like the tribe of Shem, will not be long in taking roots. They have the reputation of being hard workers but have an eye on the money, and as soon as they've made their little pile they'll want all the modern gadgets: a car, a washing machine and television set, just like the Anglo-Saxons.

'Granny has the most alarming crises which nail her in agony to her bed, then she suddenly gets better again, and just as suddenly goes wrong like an old cuckoo clock, but at times she looks so extraordinarily youthful that I am utterly confused. She takes so long to unstiffen herself in the morning (as it is she is obliged to sleep half dressed) that I run down as soon as I wake up to let the chickens out. Then I make some coffee and toast some bread and hurry upstairs again to put on the seven o'clock news and eat breakfast quietly in bed with my animals round me. Here is a story worthy of Mme de Sévigné. A lady with a house and a large garden on the outskirts of a neighbouring village, feeling herself growing old, divided her considerable fortune between her children and her grandchildren. When she fell ill all of them found excuses not to come, just as in the story of the wedding guests in the New Testament. One was off on a journey, the other was without a maid, another couldn't leave her husband and so on. The old lady, therefore, was dragged off to hospital, and there she died—all alone!

'I implore you to come if only for a few days before I return to London. We will choose Granny's television set together, the largest and best so that at least she can rediscover some of the pleasure she had in London from going to the cinema. The evenings here drag on interminably. Granny's conversation when not acid is spiced with pain and cortisone. I also am beginning to diagnose all sorts of imaginary ills, which before long are likely to become real ones. I need to be shaken up. Our poor friend Bayard is slowly recovering from his serious illness, and I'm not sure that he ought not to feel grateful for what at first alarmed his wife so much, for now they are living quietly in the little house they have built for themselves. If he had not fallen ill they might never have had time to enjoy it. He is not supposed to do anything the least strenuous, but he dragged some sand up from the *plage* to put in a corner of his garden so that his grandchildren can come and play on it.

'Je t'embrasse tendrement,

'Mé.'

Reading these letters over again, I was surprised how little I talked about my mother, and I am forced to the conclusion that our relationship was too finely balanced to be included even in these intimate letters to my husband. There is nothing extant, therefore, to allow me to describe the anguish and yet the relief I experienced upon leaving her. I should add that my husband did come over for a few days and that we did buy the most modern television set. This also gave considerable satisfaction to Brigitte, my farmer's daughter, who could now come along and discuss with my mother all the wonders she had seen in their bedroom the night before. But when I set off for the bus that was to take me to Le Havre, my conscience was not at rest. The long dark winter lay ahead, and my mother would be all alone in the house.

2

IN January I flew from London to Paris to see two young women much in the news, Sophia Loren and Juliette Gréco. I found the first trying on dresses and the second writing her memoirs. In character diametrically opposed, both seemed glad in the quiet of their respective homes to relax for a moment and look back critically on the relatively few years which had sufficed to bring them wealth and fame. Juliette Gréco had just come back from a tour of Japan, and was on the point of leaving for Rome, I think. Sophia Loren was flying to New York for the week-end. So much success, such staggering vitality, such a zest for living, combined to make me feel that my occasional sorties into the world were worse than ridiculous by comparison. The trouble about meeting such illustrious young women is that one inevitably feels small. In Normandy I had dreamed of a certain freedom. In London I had allowed myself a moment of elation. Here in Paris I was dejected by my unimportance.

Left to myself during an entire week-end I suddenly remembered a vague promise to telephone Anny Blatt who, though she is of my mother's generation, had what my mother did not have: the good health and the immense will-power to turn early misfortunes to excellent account. After an inauspicious start trundling round knitting designs in a suitcase, she rose to become one of the world's greatest experts on knitted goods and head of her own important firm in the Boulevard Malesherbes. Imagine a little woman with bright, aggressive eyes and a very animated face, whose burning enthusiasm for everything to do with her trade almost overpowers one. She is like a piece of mechanism so tightly wound up that you feel that nothing can ever stop her. I have inherited, heaven knows from whom, a cult for materials. I enthuse over those rolls of cotton, silk and man-made fibres one sees in the great department stores. It is as if I were particularly sensitive to the work and thought put into them. I can never quite take them for granted. When they spill over their softness and colour I look at them as one might look at a rose in the garden, with a touch of surprise and wonder. And I have, in common with tens of thousands of other women, a veritable passion for knitting.

These ordinary down-to-earth tastes prevent me from being truly ambitious. I envy the Sophia Lorens and the Juliette Grécos, but I am far too content to sit at home and knit. I am an excellent example of why so few women get to the top. Their desires are too diversified. The job of being a woman is already so terribly complicated.

Anny Blatt was with a foreign buyer when I arrived. There was a sale at her place, and a senior *vendeuse* came to show me round. She told me, as if it were something highly confidential, that there were some beautiful camel-hair coats, and that it was rare that these should be included in a sale. She added pontifically: 'No elegant woman could possibly not have one.' Without claiming to be elegant, I felt aggrieved. I do not own a camel-hair coat. Therefore there was something wrong with my taste. 'They are very expensive,' said the *vendeuse*, 'even in a sale.'

I tried one on and disliked myself in it, but this *vendeuse* had been *vendeuse* in some of the greatest *couture* houses in Paris. Though I shall probably never own one she has upset my preconceived views. It just shows how one can be influenced.

Anny Blatt, rid of her foreign buyer, was darting towards

me: 'Forgive me, my dear. I'm overwhelmed with work, and my daughter Annie is off to New York for the week-end.'

'What, another one?' I exclaimed. 'So is Sophia Loren!'

'And why not?' said Anny Blatt. 'It's quicker and easier than when I have to go to Roanne to visit a mill.'

She began straightway to give me all the news about her trade. Knitting was undergoing a great modification. Professional knitters didn't want to knit with fine wool any more. The thicker the wool the more they were assured of success. This was the age of the pullover and skirt. Everything was in fashion—cashmere, mohair, orlon. Yes, business was wonderful! I must come and spend Sunday afternoon with her at her house in the country. She would telephone. Her son-in-law, Marcel Stern, would be coming along after tea on his way to Orly, where Annie would be arriving after her week-end in New York.

Sunday morning was cold and dry. I went to the Russian church in the Rue Daru, which was so crowded that it was difficult to get near the icons. What surprised me was the number of children. Afterwards I lunched, still alone, in a small restaurant in the Rue Clement Marot. As the spring collections were about to start there were many foreigners there, and it was not long before my neighbours introduced themselves. There was a young woman journalist from a fashion magazine in Düsseldorf. She was pretty but her expensive-looking hat sat too heavily on her fair head and lacked the *chic* she had doubtless come to drink in thirstily during the coming marathon of fashion shows. Her French was rasping to the ear, but she was so happy to be in Paris that her faults were easily forgiven. My other neighbour was an American buyer, who watched and listened to us for some time. He was clearly anxious for feminine companionship however brief, and explained that he too had come for the collections though not to buy dresses. He was on the look-out for accessories, scarves, costume jewellery, umbrellas and all those other important items which women not only buy for themselves but receive as gifts from their menfolk. He listed for our benefit such items as Chanel bracelets and fobs and the silk Hermés squares which are all popular in New York.

When we reached the coffee stage the *patron*, while maintaining his air of geniality, began casting anxious looks in our direction in the hope that it would not be long before he could dispose of our tables. The group of hungry customers waiting to be accommodated was already large for this restaurant, which enjoys quite a reputation in this quarter frequented by the theatre, dressmaking and magazine worlds, and is famous for its *plats du jour* and steaks. The swing doors never stop turning. From time to time the man who sells sea foods which he displays outside, appetizingly arranged on damp seaweed, arrives with a plate of oysters or a lobster.

I was no sooner back at the Plaza Athénée than Anny Blatt telephoned. She had been lunching with the writer Marcelle Auclair, and was now anxious to see me arrive at her home where she was already baking a cake for tea. I was to take a local train from the Gare de Lyon. There was a twenty-minute service.

I took the tube at the Alma and, on emerging at the Gare de Lyon, experienced a moment of nostalgia for the Midi and all those small towns whose sun-burned names brought evocations of olive trees, tomatoes and cicadas. In the compartment of my train there was only one other woman, the passengers being young soldiers. The woman, who was pretty, wore a sealskin coat and a black hat. I was vexed because she was reading a book and I felt like talking. As soon as the train left the station, I decided to precipitate matters by breaking into her reading to say: 'Madame, I am afraid I may easily go past my destination. Perhaps you will be good enough to tell me when I get there?'

'That will be a pleasure,' she said, looking up for the first time from her novel. 'I myself am bound for Maison-Alfort.'

As if this were not enough, I asked her to tell me the name of the book in which she was engrossed.

'One of Dostoyevsky's novels,' she answered. 'The one called *Marie*.'

'I do not know it,' I said.

'I might not have come across it myself', she said, 'if my daughter had not written a university thesis on it. She was studying Russian, and not only did she translate this book but she also analysed it from every angle. I am obliged, alas, to read it in French. My daughter has now married a young man in the Consular service who studied Russian at the same time as she did. After their marriage they spent four years in Russia where they were extremely happy.'

I felt that my tenacity in making her talk was rewarded. On reaching my destination I took a cab to the White Cottage where Anny Blatt was waiting for me at the garden gate. Beside her was Sophie, her grey poodle. We entered her home by the kitchen.

'I am alone on Sundays,' she said. 'My chauffeur will neither work in the house nor drive the car. He says that he must spend Sunday with his own family. I told him that his sentiments seemed reasonable enough, and that I would engage somebody else to come just on Sundays. At my age I can indulge myself. But no, this proved impossible for a whole number of stupid reasons which I do not need to enumerate. 'And so, my dear Madeleine, I could not give myself the pleasure of sending the car to fetch you in Paris. You had to take the tube and that slow train from the Gare de Lyon. Do please forgive me.'

Her little house, as white as its name implies, charmed me. The kitchen was a dream.

'I have lost some of my enthusiasm for making it pretty,' she said. 'One evening not so long ago on my return from Paris I found my cottage ransacked. There was nothing left. My Persian carpets had been rolled up and taken away, even my television set had gone. The electric current was cut off and the whole affair was clearly the work of an expert gang. I was aware that other houses in the vicinity had received this treatment, but as long as a thing has not happened to one personally one is convinced that there's no real danger. My cottage for quite a time lost much of its charm for me. I might even say that it filled me with horror and fear—only now is peace slowly coming back.'

Seated opposite each other at a low table we drank tea and ate a huge apple flan to the very last crumb.

'As soon as I get home on a Friday night', said Anny Blatt, 'I start to make the pastry for the week-end. Immediately friends telephone to announce their arrival, I make a fruit pie in their honour, so that when they come into the kitchen the pastry is still warm—and the whole house is sweet with the smell of it. There is an air of welcome.

I returned to Paris by the way I had come.

At the tube station I stood for a moment in front of the indicator to discover what line I had to take. As I stood there trying to understand the complicated inter-crossing of coloured lines, a North African pushed up against me, and using the French 'thou' asked huskily:

'Tu vas bien?'

'Oui, et toi?'

'Moi je vais bien mais tu as l'air triste.'

I was not precisely sad but anxious. The North Africans had with some truth the reputation of being dangerous for those who crossed them. The passage leading to the trains was long and at this moment empty. I tried to look friendly and unconcerned. This produced another query.

'Où vas-tu?' he asked. 'Je peux venir avec toi.'

There was something childish in his remark: 'I could come with you.' The way he put it there was no compulsion, no coercion. He *could* come with me—presumably if it were what I wanted. But his dark eyes were cruel and insistent, and I remembered what my women friends had told me.

'Où vas-tu?' he repeated.

'Chez moi,' I said cautiously.

Now people appeared in view. A train could be heard arriving. I would take it even if it was going in the wrong direction. My North African did not try to follow me. His dark, questioning eyes alone remained to haunt me.

In London I fell once more into the enjoyment of the dull days. My existence lacked achievement and there were days when I hated myself for allowing the hours to fly away so uselessly. But it was precisely because nothing happened that I was happy. I was not faced with the responsibility of making decisions. I possessed that elusive thing which so many career women dream about, the right to do just as I pleased in my own home; and even if I lacked the satisfaction of a young child to look after there was Didi, my Pekinese, to amuse, to feed, to take out into the Green Park. I felt that he needed me.

My mother's letters did little to reassure me about her health. I had made her promise to write once a week. When her letter did not come, or when it was late, I became moody. I began by telling myself that Mme Javault who called for the eggs on Friday might have forgotten to post it, or she might not have time every Friday to go to the village, in which case my mother's letter would remain at the bottom of her shopping basket until Saturday or even Sunday. There might be a postal strike. There were so many in France at that time that our newspapers did not mention them. Few lasted more than twenty-four hours, but they played strange tricks with the mail. Letters sometimes arrived ten days late. I had nightmares. I was always having these frightening dreams that undid all the good of my quiet, uneventful days. When my mother's letters did arrive they generally increased my despair. They would begin by giving me news of the hens: 'I had ten eggs today. The cold is still intense. I'm doing as well as can be expected. Affectionately, Granny.' I would say to myself: 'At any rate, she's no worse. I don't need to go for a week or two. Let's wait and see what the next letter says.'

The windows of my apartment overlook the courtyard. Cars and taxis come in and out all day filling my lungs with the acrid poison of their exhausts. One must learn to accept the disadvantages of progress. If I go out by the back entrance I find myself in the centre of Shepherd Market, a picturesque vestige of old London where I can do all my shopping in slippers, so to speak. I am even willing to suffer the abominable taxi fumes in order to enjoy the convenience of being able to run out for a loaf of bread, a lamb cutlet or a pound of sugar. There is also Anna's tiny haberdashery shop, which looks as if it might have been spirited away from a nineteenth-century picture book of village life in England.

Anna is the daughter of Santarelli, a legendary *maître d'hôtel* at London's Savoy Hotel, in the restaurant that overlooks the Embankment gardens, the Thames and Cleopatra's Needle. Much appreciated by the European smart set between the wars he survived by only a few years the world in which he had shown such abundant faith and which came to such a sad end on 1st September 1939. Anna has his good looks, and when I look into her dark eyes I see her father once again and remember a whole phase of a half-forgotten Europe—Chaliapin, Guitry, the Duke of Westminster and that Prince of Wales who so dramatically gave up a throne. I also see performers on the rising floor doing strange and clever cabaret turns, people dancing in evening dress, others wearing paper hats on New Year's Eve and Derby night. I see other pictures in Anna's eyes. I see myself, for instance, when I was barely twenty, at the cash desk of the Savoy hairdressing saloon with Santarelli, so tall he always stooped a little, passing by and telling me about his baby girl. These were the Georgian days when people talked about the incipient wonder of artificial silk, crystal sets for picking up the scratchy programmes from 2LO, police raids on bottle clubs, *thè-dansants* with the blues, the tango and the Charleston. In Piccadilly Circus old women wearing shawls and black straw hats with hatpins still sold flowers at the foot of Eros. They have long since gone, and yet the other day in a Number 6 bus I sat beside a flower seller who was putting silver paper round the stalks of white heather. Her old twisted fingers would dive into a big black bag, bring out a small square of silver paper and wrap it round a twig of heather with amazing speed.

'You are very nimble with your fingers,' I said.

'I have to be, dearie,' she answered. 'The housework takes so much time that I have to make up all my best sprigs of white heather in the bus.'

A letter I found from my mother on my return from the Green Park early in March was more alarming. It was dated 27th February, and I have it in front of me now. It was an unusually long letter for Matilda, written in a surprisingly clear hand on a full quarto sheet, but having a second letter dated '28th February—8 a.m.' written crossways on the back.

What frightened me was the sudden realization that she could no longer cross the farmyard to open the stable doors where she kept her fowls. She wrote:

'I am waiting for Georgette [the farmer's young wife] to come and let the chickens out. The wind is so bitter that I caught a chill and can't move. It's as if there was a pack of ice on my back. I was so proud of being able to open the stable doors every morning. It was a little thing but it meant so much to me. And now this has happened. Sunday was the date. I feel better today but I don't dare cross the yard.

'Georgette is at my least call. There is nothing she will not do. I've not seen Patsy for three weeks. It appears that her mother has had a slight stroke. Mme Pétrel, who kept the bazaar in the centre of the village, took half an hour to die, a kindly death. From diabetes. Her shop will presumably be sold. I am doing everything I possibly can to carry on alone so that you don't need to come over. Mlle Guérin has gone to live at Honfleur. M. le Curé has left the village.

'*Wednesday, 8 a.m.* Snow is falling heavily and everything is white. It's terrible. I'm wondering if Georgette will be able to come. And what about Mme Javault? What I fear is that it starts to freeze.'

There was another letter:

'The weather is appalling. The snow and a bitter wind have finally got the better of me. Georgette is obliged to come twice a day and I am fearful lest she grows tired of doing so much, for she is busier than ever at the farm. David Owen came to see me yesterday in better health than ever in spite of his great age. I was so tired that I had to send him away. It appears that Mme Owen is better.

'*Later.* I fear that you will have to get ready to come. My health deteriorates from day to day. I wanted so much to hold out a little longer.

'I don't know what else to tell you. I am miserable to be

such a burden. There is nothing else to say. Je vous embrasse. Granny.'

Then this postscript:

'My two last nights have been horrible. It would be wiser that you should come.'

I took the Southampton–Le Havre boat train from Waterloo on a Friday night. I was unhappy enough to be glad of the distraction afforded me by the conversation of a group of men who took possession of my 'No Smoking' compartment. They belonged to a shipping company, and for the first part of the journey they discussed in technical language certain aspects of their profession which intrigued me. Men speak a different language when they are together. They exchanged information about where they left their cars when they were at sea. They mentioned various streets in Liverpool where it was safe to park a car for the duration of a round trip to the Pacific Ocean. The important thing was to remember where you had left it before a particular voyage. One described how a policeman had stopped him on a certain evening to congratulate him on the careful way in which he was driving. 'You are an example to others,' he was told. 'I have been watching you. You are prudent and you give all the right signals.' Unfortunately he had spoilt the effect by answering: 'It's only because I'm drunk.'

From the decks of the Le Havre boat I saw the *France* paying a courtesy call to Southampton. Henceforth I would be able to see her when she was in Le Havre from the bedroom window of my farm. My stewardess asked me for news of my husband, and I asked her for news of her children. She said that her son was an officer on a Blue Star ship and that her daughter was a nurse.

'They earn a lot of money,' she said, 'but they never seem

to have enough. To think that when I was newly married my husband and I had to manage on £4 a week.'

She detailed her budget, mentioning £1 for housekeeping and £1 put away for holidays or illness. She remembered that coal cost 4s. 10d. a sack. Alas, people are always looking back over their shoulders to the days of their youth. We never learn the uselessness of it.

At Le Havre a customs officer made me open all my bags. He said that he was sorry but that it was the law. I wondered what he hoped to find, but in the end he gave me an ingratiating smile. The two women customs officers were not there. Both are war widows. The one who usually greets me was probably in her native Brittany where her daughter, Yvette, after difficult examinations, had just become a schoolmistress. She spent Christmas with her mother at Le Havre. I had heard all about it when last I came through.

'"Mother," she said, at the end of the holidays, "it has been lovely to be with you and Granny, but I have missed the children in my class. I love them so much!"'

'When she told me that', said her mother, 'I realized that I would have to ask for a transfer to be near her. I am so glad she likes her work. Being fond of one's work is important.'

Remembering all this, I asked my customs officer, who by now was all anxiety to please, what had happened to Mme Le Moing.

'She is at the sheds where the *France* comes in,' he said.

'And her colleague, the other woman customs officer?' I asked.

'She is ill,' he answered.

I had learned a good deal about her also in the course of my many journeys through Le Havre. Her two sons had become brilliant civil engineers, and I remember her saying to me: 'As far as they are concerned I have nothing more to worry about. But that will not prevent me from going on working. It is to keep my independence, you understand. One should never become a burden to one's children.'

So I said to the *douanier*: 'What is the matter with her?'

'There has been a tragedy,' he answered. 'We don't even know if she'll come back. Her eldest son put some film negatives in his stove one evening wanting to burn them. Then when he had finished his work he went to bed. They found him dead in the morning. He had been asphyxiated. His mother is distracted.'

Our coach rolled in the direction of Tancarville through the half-light of early morning. At Tancarville we picked up the usual school children bound for Honfleur. A boy of about twelve was waiting for us at the head of a dozen other children, and he was smoking a cigarette like a Cadi. He led his friends to a seat at the rear of the coach without so much as looking at the girls. A little boy was standing by the driver. There is room for half a dozen people to stand by the wide windscreen. They are generally the *habitués* who supply Monsieur André, our driver, with local gossip.

After about ten minutes Monsieur André said to the little boy: 'At the next stop you will see an old woman with some parcels. She is always waiting for us on Saturday morning. You will jump out smartly and help her.'

'Very well,' said the child.

This lesson in politeness intrigued me. It reflected another age and savoured of the children's story books of Victorian times. Our driver never missed an opportunity to instil good principles into the children he drove to and from school. When the coach stopped there was the old woman waiting, her bundles at her feet. The little boy jumped down to help her in. He was blushing—partly because he knew that the people in the coach had their eyes on him, partly because he was proud to have been singled out by André for this important work. The woman's legs were swollen and the bandages were visible through her coarse stockings. We made way for her so that she could sit by the door, but it took her several minutes to climb in. I kept on thinking of my mother. Massive doses of cortisone were having that sort of effect on her. Her once beautiful legs were at times grotesquely swollen.

The clock in front of the Mairie showed that it was just past nine when we arrived at Villers. I went to pick up my car at the garage. Patsy was waiting for me. She was concerned about my mother. She also had worries of her own. Mme Owen, as my mother had informed me in her last letter, had suffered a slight stroke. We could sympathize with each other. Our mothers had almost become children again and they needed us.

My sense of guilt about those heavy doses of cortisone was revived. But I told myself that it was that or being paralysed. I was always telling myself this. I had to make peace with myself. And what would another daughter have done when the possibility of taking away pain resides in a box of pills?

When I entered the farmhouse hope came surging up inside me. A boiling fowl was cooking on the Aga stove. My mother was obviously delighted to see me. But when I saw how fantastically her poor legs were swollen I was overcome by panic. How strangely the mind works on such occasions! I found myself recalling that when I was twenty I used to think that in many ways she was prettier than I was. Not only did the turn of her ankles and the smallness of her feet impress me but also her hips—they were less conspicuous than mine. I am always worrying about the size of my hips. I envy girls who can wear clothes off the peg. The elegant thing is to be thin as a broomstick.

Things didn't go too badly that first day.

She admired the teddy bear I had brought for Patsy's baby and some tiny red shoes from Harrods. I had also brought presents for Brigitte, my farmer's little daughter, to whom I had become very attached. Jacques Déliquaire, my farmer, was the younger son of that Déliquaire whom we all used to call the Père, a tall Viking of a man, speaking pure Norman, whom I described in *Madeleine Young Wife* when he became my tenant farmer after the liberation of Paris. The Père and his wife, Madeleine (we used to bake cakes for each other on our name day), had now retired and were acting as caretakers in a villa down by the sea. I had given Jacques part of my land when he came back from doing his military service in Indo-China. He had just married a local girl, Georgette, and I was able to set them up at Berlequet, a beautiful little farmhouse, which Victor Duprez had sold me the previous year. This modernly equipped farm, so pretty and feminine, had been designed by Victor Duprez's wife, Simone, and had something of Marie Antoinette's Petit Trianon. The low house, stables, garages and barns, all fitted with electric light, were colourful and doll-like. The farmhouse in which the Père had lived and brought up his two sons was not mine. He had rented my orchards without living on my land. The Père had a tremendously colourful personality, and my husband forgave him all his crafty ways for the joy of hearing him speak with that rich imagery, which farmers on that same land must have employed four centuries ago. He had once worked on a millionaire's stud farm at Deauville, knew all about racehorses, and always found an excuse for leaving his work and going to the races during the season at Deauville.

I was glad now that the Père had retired to have young farmers of my own living on my own land. I had known Jacques as a little boy coming home from school across my orchard with a satchel over his back. It seemed right that Berlequet should go to him. But I did not give my heart away too quickly. I was beginning to have a long experience of the Balzacian streak which, in spite of a changing world, can still be found in certain of our Norman tenant farmers. Jacques and Georgette had their fairy-tale farmhouse at a nominal rent but, in order not to be too generous until I had tested them, I kept back a tiny part of the long low house— two rooms to be exact, which, like all the others, opened directly on the garden. I did not seriously intend to inflict lodgers on them, nor even friends, though by contract I had the right to do so. I wanted a lever for possible use against their future behaviour.

I had known and liked this place long before Simone Duprez rebuilt it. When the Germans overran France it was a hovel—though a pretty one. A giant called Groscol lived there.

Jacques and Georgette did not complain about the two rooms I kept back. Other things I did must have occasionally vexed them. They remained patient and polite. We were putting each other through a long series of adaptability tests. Jacques, though less picturesque than his father, had the advantage of having seen the world. He too wanted the experiment to work, and he knew how to go about it. A young man does not spend several years in the Far East without acquiring a certain amount of wisdom. There was also his young wife, who had many of the qualities I most admire. We were bound to get along well together. When Brigitte was born I suddenly had what I most wanted—a little girl to spoil and amuse.

But the bringing of our two families to complete understanding remained a delicate task. There was one particularly difficult problem which was bound in a roundabout way to have an effect on my mother's happiness. That is why I realized from the very beginning how vital it was that I should make the right decision. At the time it seemed almost beyond my ability.

The Père had not yet retired, but his health was failing rapidly and the matter was urgent. He needed a successor, a young farmer with enough cash to buy the stock and walk right into this rich inheritance. If things had been different he might have turned to his elder son Roger, but for a number of reasons Roger had broken away from life on the farm. He had married Jeaninne Trémois, a village girl, and was making a comfortable living by driving a truck for Mme Baudon, whose small empire included a grocery store and a building firm.

Meanwhile the Père was continually engaging some farmhand to help him with those tasks he was no longer strong enough to do himself. None seemed satisfactory until a young man called Rémi arrived.

Rémi, like his namesake the Évêque of Rheims, was an ambitious man. He worked hard, and what is more he worked supremely well. When he promised to do a thing it was done quickly and to perfection. So, as you can imagine, he became the sun, the moon and the stars to the Père and to Madeleine Déliquaire, whose two sons had now left the paternal roof. Rumour soon had it that Rémi planned to take over the Père Déliquaire's farm. Now this was of vital importance to me for the following reason.

The orchard in which my house stands is one of the richest in grass in the region, and for that alone is much coveted. The cider apples are also of the best. Because of my long and most friendly association with the Père I had allowed him to go on renting the grass and cider apple crop of this one large orchard at the time Jacques took over my land. A stream divided it from the orchards which the Père cultivated. In short it was delightfully, if not vitally, important to him.

So my role in the Père's succession suddenly became

large. It became even larger when the Père and Rémi together decided to approach me with a proposition. Rémi had no money. The Père needed to be paid immediately for his cows and the rest of his stock. Would I either finance him or guarantee the very large loan that, with my backing, Rémi could obtain from the Crédit Agricole?

I could not easily dismiss this appeal. The Père was an old friend and I much respected young Rémi. M. Sandret, who owned most of the land which the Pé, as we sometimes called him, rented, together with his farmhouse, was quite willing to transfer the lease to the new arrival. I had no valid reason to refuse. In fact diplomatically I would be gaining a powerful ally to the east of my possessions and, like Marie-Thérèse, I would have friends on both frontiers.

On the other hand, now that the Père was leaving the land and handing it over to a stranger might there not be a moral obligation to benefit Jacques, who was not only his son but also my farmer? Our friendship, so carefully built up, might break on this dangerous reef. In the end, instead of having two friends I might find myself with two discontented families.

At that time it would amuse me to take a milk can and go to fetch my milk every morning at Berlequet. It gave me a short walk and I felt like someone in a story book. The country was so entirely unspoilt by progress that I would never have been surprised to meet an ogre or the *chat botté*. Georgette was as affectionate as ever; her daughter was adorable and I used to invent new games every day to amuse her. I gave her story books in English, and she seldom forgot a word I taught her.

Georgette and I did not often discuss the grave events taking place at the Pé's home, but on one occasion I remember her saying: 'The Père does what he pleases. Just now it's Rémi this and Rémi that—and now that Rémi is married and his wife is expecting a baby, there's the amusement of a new family. I don't deny that Jacques and I are sometimes a little envious. If the Père's farm is a good one it's a great deal thanks to Jacques and Roger who did so much of the work when they were children and unpaid. Roger has left the land so he doesn't count any more, but Jacques is just beginning to set up for himself and—well . . . I'm not saying that we could afford to buy the Père's cows or his farm implements—Jacques is still paying instalments on his tractor which cost him a million francs.

In all this neither Georgette nor Jacques ever sought to discover what role I might have decided to play, and for the time being I didn't myself know. I was, of course, aware that matters of this kind assume tremendous proportions in country districts, especially districts as medieval in outlook as ours. In cities one is accustomed to hearing about large sums of money. The value of the Pé's twenty cows would have been negotiated by a city broker in a matter of minutes, but here we dealt in cows, plus the human element, and this required a pre-1914 European diplomacy.

I remember that particular summer as being hot. The vegetables in my kitchen garden were rare, but Matilda, who was then still able to get about a little, and who had green fingers, had produced some splendid lettuces, and I spent long, quiet, pleasant hours cosseting the strawberry beds or digging up potatoes. As I worked I thought about the Pé and Rémi, and whether or not I should give my bond and help to lay the foundations for this new empire.

Fortunately my husband chose this precise moment to come over from London for a week. We had a wonderful time. The day he was to fly back was also the day that I needed to take my important decision about our coveted orchard. Rémi, convinced that I would allow my arrangement with the Père to be taken over automatically by himself, had already put his cows to graze round our house. If I made no protest he would benefit from the law of usage. The matter had become urgent.

My husband made the decision for me. We were sitting at the top of the orchard in my car and he said: 'You must have one farmer and he must be Jacques. A house divided can only fall. Don't try to be a diplomat. They invariably mess things up.'

So we sent for Jacques and told him the news. And we told him that not only could he have our home orchard on a proper nine years' lease, but that he could have the two rooms we had kept back at Berlequet, and that we would call on the notary that very evening to have him draw up the necessary papers.

Jacques was delighted in a dignified way. Georgette said apropos the two rooms: 'Oh, madame, you make me very happy. This way Brigitte will have a room of her own.'

We had brought joy into their home. That was the easiest part. The messenger who brings good news is always welcome. The difficult part remained to be done. We had to go over to the Père's farm to tell Rémi and his young wife that we were taking away from them the best orchard in their establishment.

Sadly we crossed the stream.

The house was closed, but we heard voices in the distance and the clatter of pails and milk churns. Soon we saw a procession coming towards us which might have been a picture from a Bible story: Rémi and his young wife Christianne, and between them the donkey with the heavy milk churns strapped on either side of the saddle. Rémi and his wife were beautiful to look at, young and all smiles. I felt miserable knowing how we were going to hurt them. Not only would they lose their most valuable orchard, but Jacques, in a sense their rival, would be getting it.

Christianne had a rosy freshness and her youth was warm like a midday sun. She was not yet twenty. It was she who went into the house first, and she went immediately to fetch her sleeping baby to show it to me, bringing it me so trustingly.

My husband turned to Rémi to inform him of the reason of our visit. Rémi turned white, and suddenly I saw Christianne sobbing against the cheek of her newborn. At that moment I felt so miserable that I hated myself. I began to cry in unison with Christianne, and Robert, afraid of the consequences and fearing that I might go back on my word to Jacques, cut short this lamentable meeting. Feeling almost ashamed of ourselves we slowly recrossed the stream.

This decision, cruel as it seemed at the time, had a vital bearing on the story I am trying to tell. Georgette now took my mother under her wing. Relations between the two houses became extremely close. The two rooms at Berlequet could not have been more appreciated. The whole aspect of the farmhouse changed. The parents' bedroom became a sitting-room. The sleeping quarters were transferred to the new wing. Brigitte's bedroom, with her little bed and all her toys, became a thing of delight. A communicating door allowed her free access to the room in which Georgette and Jacques slept. In the summer honeysuckle looked in at the windows.

Well, as I said, that first day with Matilda passed off fairly well, except that I kept looking at her poor swollen legs and wondering what to do about them.

'The doctor wants to cut my cortisone,' she said. 'If he does, you'll see. I'll not be able to get up the next morning.'

In the evening we watched a television play. Afterwards I was so tired that I went up to my room and threw myself on the bed without even making it, but at five o'clock I woke up shaking all over. I had seen Matilda in a dream. She was being followed by a large duck, who suddenly went off to swim in a pond of filthy water. The duck caught up with her again and followed her into the house, where he had made a mess on the newly washed tiles, his droppings expanding until they formed a huge circle.

Frightened by what this might portend, I rushed downstairs, where I found my mother stretched on the black-and-white tiles of her bedroom floor. As her hands no longer had any strength in them she couldn't get up, and she must have been calling me for more than an hour. She had wanted to go to the toilet. I tried to lift her up, but every time I touched her she yelled with pain. The floor was soaked. I kept on slipping, and as the grey dawn of this terrible morning broke I thought I would fall myself and be unable to get up. At last I succeeded in raising her on to the bed, but the piercing cries she let out terrified me. Could she have broken anything?

When the doctor arrived he said that her heart was strong. So were her lungs. Did he want to give her courage? She would have none of it.

'I want to die!' she said. 'I have suffered too much and too long!'

I spent two days washing. There was no longer any question of leaving her alone at night. Her room was next to the kitchen. I snatched short bouts of sleep on a sofa in the living-room. Trying to put her on a bed pan gave her such agony, her entire body being a mass of pain, that it made me panic. I lived in an atmosphere of horror and impotence.

I would jump into the car to shop in the village. My shopping list contained a host of prescriptions written out by the doctor, possibly to ease his conscience, for I fear that they did my mother little good. All these injections, medicaments and medicines were fantastically expensive, and my bills at the chemist's were greater than those for all the rest of the house. Sometimes I would make a hurried call at Montauzan where my friend Patsy was as tired and anxious as I was. Her mother's right arm and leg were paralysed, but she had no pain, and in her misfortune seemed almost happy to be with her daughter and her grandchildren.

More than a month had gone by since this partial stroke, and she gave the impression of having come to terms with it. She was reading again many of the novels which had most excited her when she was young. Those of Elinor Glyn brought back sunny days, and one afternoon she said to me: 'Why yes, I am happy, for this is the first time that I have really enjoyed the company of my daughter and my grandchildren. My son-in-law also is goodness itself. See what a multitude of things he does to give me pleasure!' Her bed had the prettiest covering and a simple device of cords hung from the ceiling to help her sit up. He had also made her a special card table, for like so many of her generation she was mad about bridge. When Patrick, the eldest of the Poirot children, came back from college to spend Thursday, their day off, at home he would organize a game for her. I asked if she was not disappointed in some of the novels that must have seemed so fresh and daring when she was a girl, but she answered: 'No. I find them just the same and they give me no less pleasure. There's no reason why a good love story should ever grow old. The details that change such as dress make no difference at all. If Patsy and you could suddenly find yourself transported into the Edwardian period, and have to wear the clothes we wore then, you would need less than a week to feel thoroughly at home in them. It might even 'feel strange to come back to the present. No, the fundamentals are what matter, and for a young woman love is the thing that counts. Love is what she dreams about whether there are horse-drawn omnibuses or sputniks.'

Patsy had drawn her mother's white hair severely back from the forehead. This gave her quite a different appearance, an eighteenth-century Pompadour look. These short moments at Montauzan kept me sane, for when we were

alone Patsy and I exchanged confidences. Indeed we were
not afraid to tell each other our most secret thoughts. There
were times when we told ourselves that we were realists. To
have one's mother ill at home changes one's entire outlook.
It would be foolish to deny that one doesn't often feel
impatient.

Patsy's paternal uncle, David Owen, was eighty, and so
vigorous that he was always planting or digging in the
garden or striding through the village. His pleasures consisted in a radio to listen to the news in English, his *Daily
Telegraph*, which came to him every morning from London,
and an occasional cup of English tea at the farm. He lived in
a world in which Mrs Patrick Campbell and Mr Bernard
Shaw had their places.

My mother, it will be recalled, had told him one day when
he looked in at the farm that she was too tired to talk to him.
In fact, he had found her prostrate with pain, whereupon,
to amuse her, he gave a comic account of his 'amazing'
bravery in getting himself vaccinated that week against
smallpox, of which there was an epidemic in England. In
fact, of course, he is the bravest possible man, having in
his youth taken part in the deadly campaign of the Dardan-
elles. In those days he nearly died from malaria and dysen-
tery; but it put the envious Matilda into a fury and she
had sent him packing. She couldn't bear to see this man,
whom she judged useless, in such maddeningly good health
while she writhed in agony.

'I understand your mother,' said Mrs Owen when I told
her this story. 'He came to me too just after my stroke to
tell me some story about his vaccination. I was furious.
What's a little scratch on the arm compared to the complete
paralysis of it? Besides, it isn't fair. A man can idle away his
hours. But a woman has so much she ought to be doing. I,
for instance, ought to be helping Patsy in the house and
knitting baby clothes for my grandson. Oh, it makes me

mad!' She laughed her bright, youthful laugh and added: 'Men become very selfish when they grow old. Old men and children think about nothing but themselves.'

On my way out I found David in the sitting-room sitting like a pasha in front of his afternoon tea, and the sight of him there reminded me of something the Begum Aga Khan once said to me apropos her own parents.

'There's nothing quite so difficult as looking after one's mother when she is ill. Looking after one's father is quite another thing. Fathers allow themselves to be cosseted like pashas!'

Even when David is in the room the family speak French, and David does not mind in the least. He has never made the slightest effort to learn the language. France and the French are merely accessories in his well-organized existence. Every Wednesday Patsy takes him in her small car to Trouville where he buys a loaf of brown bread, some fruit, a lottery ticket, his favourite English soap and seeds to plant in the garden. He is one of the most contented men I know. And it is his utter blissfulness that puts our mothers in such a rage. These women, whose fingers are so cunning when sewing, knitting and cooking, are suddenly consumed with envy. They say to themselves: 'If we could only do this or that, the house would hum. Experience has taught us so much and now suddenly our knowledge is useless because of the paralysis in our hands.'

I cannot blame my mother for sending David home. I too, alas, am of an envious nature. This trait, as far as I am concerned, reared up its ugly head when I was at school. I was madly envious of a girl who had learnt to whistle like a thrush. Later I envied girls who could sing, dancers both classical and ballet and, of course, girls of outstanding beauty or intelligence. Contented girls must be rare, for on the whole a girl is much more ambitious than a boy. As one grows older it's good health that one envies, and women like Patsy's mother or my mother wanted above all to remain independent to the end of their days. Not to be dependent on their daughter—Matilda was always saying it. So was Mrs Owen. And now the thing they most feared had happened.

Mrs Owen was not afraid to talk of her own misfortune. I asked her one day: 'How did the stroke happen? Were you conscious of it at the time?'

'You must know', she answered, 'that when I am in Paris I spend much of every day paying calls. The fact that I was widowed young made me cultivate my friends and I still keep up with them, and not only with them but with their children and their grandchildren. And as you know I am an enthusiastic bridge player. I like to take the Métro. On this occasion I had arrived at the station where I needed to change, when I suddenly became aware that my leg had gone dead. It can happen to anybody, can't it? One takes up a wrong position and then the leg or the arm momentarily becomes numb. As you can imagine the train didn't wait for me. The doors closed, the train began to move and still I didn't get those salutory pins and needles that generally follow a moment of numbness.

'The miracle was that I did manage to get out of the train at the next station, and even drag myself to a bench, but after sitting there for a while I decided that I must at all costs get up into the streets, and this I finally managed to do. A taxi came along. I hailed it and stoically made my afternoon call. My hostess did her best to reassure me. She said that it was probably sciatica and would pass, but she asked her daughter to see me safely home, which she did.

'My Paris apartment is very comfortable, but I live alone and I don't have the telephone. The telephone has become so terribly expensive in France. After all I have no business to transact, and in my youth people got along quite well with letters. However, when there's something urgent my friends telephone the concierge, and as I've known her a long time she doesn't mind running up and giving me the message. If I mention this lack of a telephone in my flat it's because on returning home I felt vaguely anxious about what the night can sometimes bring to a person of my age living alone. One is never sure how one will feel in the morning, and though my leg did not hurt, I was worried because life did not seem to flow back into it as quickly as I expected. I hit on a very simple plan. I left the apartment door open by wedging a chair between it and the frame, telling myself that when the concierge came up the stairs in the morning to deliver the letters she would see that my door was open, and that would make her call out and ask me if I was all right.

'My night was very disturbed, and I kept on going to the toilet, but every time I got up my leg appeared less willing to obey me. When at eight o'clock the concierge came up with the mail she gave a cry of horror, imagining that my apartment had been burgled, and that I might have been murdered. I put her mind at rest on that score, but explained that my leg was getting worse and would she be good enough to telephone to Patsy.

'Patsy arrived within a few hours, and I had never been so relieved to see her. The doctor she sent for listened to my heart, seemed satisfied, and said that my blood pressure was normal, but Patsy decided that I couldn't remain alone in Paris. I must be brought to Montauzan. As my son-in-law was away on business, and as my daughter's car, as you know, is only a tiny one like your own, we decided to hire an ambulance. I made the journey comfortably, but before long my arm became as numb as my leg. I can no longer write letters to my friends, and there are moments when I am quite cast down.'

She smiled wanly, and I recalled that by a coincidence she and I had returned to London last autumn by the same Le

Havre–Southampton boat train. I had probably done rather
too much in the house, with my mother beginning to be so
helpless, and I had an attack of lumbago. The date was the
eleventh of November. Something had gone wrong with
the boat, or perhaps it was the tides. At all events we
berthed late and missed the proper train. We had to change
several times, and it was Mrs Owen who valiantly helped
me with my heavy bags. I had been amazed by the ease with
which she lifted them. Who could have foretold how swiftly
she would lose her strength? One can count neither on one's
health nor on one's fortune. To think too much about them
is to cloud the sunny days, but to take them too much for
granted is to be improvident. And what's the good of
knowing? Had I been a thousand times more aware of the
parable of the wise and the foolish virgins, I could doubtless
not have warded off the blow that was to fall upon me that
spring. All our plans are futile.

Fifille enjoyed our visits to Mrs Owen, who allowed her
to jump up on her bed, where she snored peacefully with her
head between her paws while Patsy's baby boy, Philip,
ran happily round the room hugging his teddy bear. Philip
did not talk yet, but would come to be kissed by all of us in
turn. He loved us in spite of our faults and sorrows, and we
seemed important to him, and we were grateful to him
because he made us forget our problems. His robust good
health and joyousness disproved the saying that one is too
old to have a baby at forty. Patsy declared that he was her
chef d'œuvre, and though the house was always full of
children, her own and those of her innumerable friends, he
seemed to bring it an air of added youthfulness. His older
brothers were always playing with him, and Anne, his sister,
would find a score of different ways to amuse him at meal
times. The women at Montauzan were the most nearly
happy I have ever known. There was no schedule to keep to.
Things were done when it seemed right to do them. Money

never appeared to matter. They all had just enough not to have to worry about it. Perhaps because of this I never heard anybody grumble.

Most evenings at five o'clock I would drive down to the village school to fetch Brigitte, my farmer's daughter. As soon as she recognized my tiny car by its colour and number she would rush up and throw herself into my arms. We would first go to the *plage* where we would fill a sack with dry sand. I was planting sweet peas, and somebody had advised me to add sand to the damp, black earth in my garden. This month of March was wet and cold, but the exercise warmed us, and Brigitte, Fifille and I would chase each other to the first little waves of the sea. The sands at low tide stretched out for nearly a quarter of a mile. The fact that I had two women in my life, my mother and Mrs Owen, no longer able to walk, filled me with a furious desire to run. I wanted to see how much energy I could generate, and while I was appalled by the selfishness that obviously gave rise to this desire (the same fault that my mother found so despicable in poor David) I could do nothing to repress it. I was guilty of the same joy that mourners experience on the way back from a funeral.

One evening on my return home I lay on the couch reading the saintly life of a Spanish nun. I thought that by delving into this work I might acquire a greater degree of self-sacrifice, but the book was an old one and times have changed. There is no longer even in great cities the same poverty to relieve. Nobody would thank us any more for the clothes of which we tire. The factory girl buys the same nylon slip and cotton dress as we do at Marks & Spencer's or Les Prix Unis. The story-book kindnesses of Lady Bountiful have become more than slightly ridiculous to youthful eyes, and we are all acutely aware that the State, through the money it takes from us, does it all so much better. In fact, it makes it impossible for us to open our purse, for imagine what sums one would need to come to the help of a modern family! The days of easy indulgence are over, and we must find other means to amass treasures in heaven, but I would not be surprised if many of us do not occasionally regret those far-off times when a woman with a house of her own, and a little money put away, could enjoy the luxury of being charitable.

I put down the book and went to the boiler-room. I would put the washing on a line to dry, for this weather made it difficult to hang it outside. As usual I had spent hours washing. The television announcer said that it had been raining at Nice. That at least was comforting. Towards ten o'clock I went to bed exhausted.

I would set my alarm clock every two or three hours to go down and peep at my mother. When she was asleep it was as if I saw her growing older. In sleep she abandoned the struggle, allowed herself to be carried away on the current. It was immensely sad to stand beside her in the cold hours of the night, knowing that she was drifting away to the other shore.

Mado Duprez telephoned one morning to inquire after my mother and invite me to dinner, a very simple dinner, she said, to which she was also inviting the Poirots and a M. and Mme Rouget, whom I didn't know but who had expressed a wish to meet me. She added that Mme Rouget was a South African and that she had read a number of my books.

The dinner was for the middle of the following week. I wanted to go to it, but I was worried about leaving Matilda. The frost had set in, and every morning the grass in the orchards was crisp and white. As soon as I came down I would put a kettle on the Aga for tea or coffee and then open the stable doors to let the Rhode Island Reds out. They also had a hot breakfast, warm milk poured over bread to which I added any tempting morsels collected during the previous day. They quickly became accustomed to those warm breakfasts, and it was a wonder to see them waiting so impatiently for me. I would cross the courtyard in my blue dressing-gown of Pyrenees wool which I bought at the Galeries Lafayette in Regent Street. The first time they saw me wearing this flamboyant apparel they were mightily afraid, not recognizing me from my last visit, but now they gave me a tremendous welcome. I derived enormous pleasure from our hens. Everything smelt so good on stepping out of the house, and it was fun to hear the farm-yard noises all round—our own farm, the Poulin farm, the Rémi farm and so on. I found myself increasingly remembering the stories my mother told me about herself and her sister, Marie-Thérèse, when they were both young in Paris. Marie-Thérèse, for instance, made hats for a beautiful *demi-mondaine* who had been set up by a wealthy lover in an expensive home of her own in one of the smartest quarters of Paris. Every morning this lovely woman would look out of her window, peeping through the lace curtains, and see a poor hunchback carrying a green baize sack which contained the work he was delivering to a tailor. She would poke fun at him. Then one day she called her lady's maid and told her to give the hunchback one of her jackets to alter.

'Like that he will have to come up and see me,' she said, 'and that will amuse me.'

The hunchback arrived and the lovely *demi-mondaine* put on the jacket to show him what was wrong. When he touched her, arranging the material, she suddenly felt an inner turmoil which quickly developed into an uncontrollable passion. She dismissed her lover, sold her house, the furniture and all her jewels and went to live with her hunchback in a small house on the outskirts of Paris. When her maid went to visit her she found her radiantly happy feeding her chickens! There was something of Boccaccio in this strange story, which at least had the merit of being true. Love can play the strangest tricks. These mornings when I crossed the courtyard to open the stable doors, when all the chickens were gathered in a semicircle in front of me waiting for their hot food or their grain, I thought about the *demi-mondaine* for whom my mother sewed and for whom Marie-Thérèse made hats, and I wondered if she was still alive and whether she still loved her hunchback tailor.

As soon as the hens had emptied the bowl, they all went off into the orchard where they scattered. Now the birds would come for the grain that the chickens had left. Then I would give Granny her breakfast, take mine up on a tray and go back to bed with Fifille, often just in time to put on the eight o'clock news. I would write a little until through the open windows I heard Georgette swinging the milk can. It was time to go down again. Georgette would help me fill two pails of Russian or Cardiff anthracite, and another of coke, which we would bring back into the house. She would tell me all the village news and now, because we were getting to know each other better, she would confide in me her plans and her dreams. Their television set was in the bedroom and Brigitte would come and watch it until she fell asleep, but the important thing was that because of this new toy Jacques stayed at home more often in the evening. My farmers had prospered well since first I had put them in this house. Jacques was a tremendous worker whose day stretched from dawn to dusk and who never took time off, and Georgette was to him much more than the mother of his little girl. She was his partner. She helped with the hay, milked the cows and made the faggots, and he was thus able to dispense with a hired hand. Every penny they made was for them. The German tractor was a tremendous help. Jacques even managed to find time to hire himself and the tractor out to neighbouring farmers who were less competent and hard working. He had a motor-car long before I was finally persuaded to buy myself my small Citroën, and in those early days he would drive down to the village in his sedan, passing me on my bicycle. But by now we had both learned many lessons. I, by not being too greedy at the beginning, had vastly strengthened my position. We knew that we could count on one another. Jacques and Georgette never failed me when I needed them, and when they wanted something they asked for it with dignity and I was always happy to give it to them. Thus, as I say, Georgette would confide in me her dreams. What were they precisely at this moment? When Jacques had finished paying for the television set Georgette would ask him for a wardrobe which would take up half the space of a wall. There would be shelves for her linen and sliding doors, and she would be able to keep her treasures under lock and key. It would depend, of course, on how the summer worked out, if the cows remained in good health, if it rained when it should do and if the sun shone at the right time, and, most important of all, if they could harvest enough hay. The desires of my farmer's wife interested me enormously, for I saw in these the continuation of life itself.

On the day of Gaston and Mado's dinner party rain fell in torrents. I went to Montauzan. There, in Mrs Owen's room, Patsy gave me a glamorous hair-do. We laughed gaily while Mrs Owen, propped up on pillows in the bed, gave us sage advice and little Philip ran in circles, falling, looking surprised, then quickly picking himself up. I had bought a new, very deep red nail varnish, but all the washing that my mother's illness necessitated had brought my hands to a deplorable condition and I was ashamed of them. Patsy, whose hands were little better than mine, thought that a generous application of varnish would deflect attention from their roughness. In order to test the colour we put the smallest dab on one of Philip's tiny nails. He looked hurt, then puzzled and rather proud. David kept coming back and forth with a wheelbarrow full of logs. Because of the rain he wore his Home Guard overcoat and he dripped from head to feet, but looked as strong and as straight as an oak tree.

I was the first to arrive at the 'Plein Air'. This beautiful house made all of us look like poor cousins. It stands in spacious grounds half way up the steep hill from the village on the way to Houlgate and Caen. The drive up to the house itself is even steeper than the road. This, of course, gives the house a commanding position with a view dominating the whole bay as far as Le Havre, but it terrifies the sort of driver I am. Nevertheless I arrived safely, parking my car neatly on the gravel.

Mado, very elegant, was seated in her beautiful drawing-room with her daughter Martine. Because it was the little girl's bedtime she had come down in a dressing-gown and slippers. Already there was much of the little woman about her. A red hair band made a splash of contrast with her mat complexion and big dark eyes. Mother and daughter made a lovely picture, almost a fashion plate. Because they were so immaculate (indeed one never saw them otherwise) I wondered what had made the tear in Martine's Norwegian slippers, but I did not need to ask. She must have noticed my quick glance, for she said: 'It's my dog—he eats everything.'

'I would have thought that he had become reasonable by now,' I said. 'We were such good friends last time I came. Indeed he jumped on my lap and went fast asleep.'

Martine's large eyes suddenly filled with tears. 'He's not the same dog,' she whispered, but after that speech failed her and her poor little face was contorted with grief.

'Fabien had an accident,' Mado explained gently. 'He was asleep on the perron one day when a friend drove up in his car. The noise must have surprised him, for he woke up with a start and rolled down right under one of the front wheels. He died on the way to the vet. Our unfortunate guest, in an effort to assuage Martine's grief, sent her another little dog, and it's he who is responsible for chewing her slippers.'

We were waiting for Gaston, who had gone to Paris on business. He would be back at any moment. M. and Mme Rouget arrived. We were introduced, and I learned that M. Rouget was mayor of a beautiful village called Douville that I knew rather well. He was also the owner of a fine orchard that bordered my land along the route to St Vaast. Now the Poirots arrived. Patsy and Jacques had been obliged to get dinner ready for their children. The two older boys had come from their *lycée* at Honfleur to spend the night at Montauzan. Philip had been bathed and put to bed. Fortunately there was no problem about finding a baby sitter. The boys would be there. I so seldom saw Patsy in a dress that it took me a moment to get used to the sight of her in this new guise. Ten minutes later Gaston came in to greet us. He looked so elegant in his well-cut suit that it was hard to believe he had just covered the long distance from Paris.

With the arrival of Gaston the conversation was spiced with the Grand Life. It was as if he had come to us from the court of Louis XV. He had the grand manner, and both his language and his gestures were precise and studied. He had a position of which there is no very clear English equivalent. He was a broker in châteaux, ancestral properties and the sort of *haras* or stud farms where Derby winners are bred. The Baron de X was increasing the size and importance of his *haras*, the Prince de X was selling his château. The huge sums at stake never seemed in tune with normal life. I was apt to forget that though France is a republic there remain deep vestiges of a monarchical system in which private fortunes and privileges are allowed to remain and to flourish. For those who, like myself, are not jealous of the riches of others this can only add a certain picturesqueness to what is happening round one. There is nothing so dull as uniformity.

The dinner, as you would guess, left nothing to be desired. Gaston had trained his wife to be the perfect hostess, and though he adored her and his daughter he would not have tolerated the slightest departure from what he considered gastronomic perfection. We were served by Georges Baudry, who wore white cotton gloves and at night acted as footman. His mother came from Brittany and used to visit my farm to pluck fowl. She was a very precise woman in every way, and she carefully bought the night-dress she wanted to be buried in, although firmly convinced that her husband would die first. In this she had been proved wrong. She was the first to die, worn out by a furious desire to put money aside.

The excellent white wine from the Loire was a gift, Gaston explained, from a client. When it came to the red wine, he said: 'I am serving you this one because I am afraid that it may spoil if I keep it too long in my cellar!'

'Then let us drink all you have of it!' somebody called out.

The dinner was very gay.

When just before midnight we got into our respective cars to drive home the rain had stopped. The village was asleep. I skirted the church and the walled presbytery garden. Our curé had been most unfortunate. He had replaced one who had spent most of his life in the village. Though he was, I think, admirable, he had the misfortune to have a little money, and some parishioners objected because he drove about in a car of his own—one which, in Europe generally, had become, because of its cost and excellence, something of a symbol. His brother, a widower, had come on a visit to recover from a serious illness. He was devotedly nursed by Mlle Lefranc, our *femme sage* and district nurse, and they had fallen in love. They were married and now lived very happily in a pretty house with a garden. Mlle Lefranc undoubtedly gained status by becoming our *curé's* sister-in-law, but the *curé* himself was not able to win over the hearts of a village population which still regretted the shepherd who had been with them so long. Or perhaps it was the more conservative who disliked him. He had another idiosyncrasy besides liking fast motor-cars. He took pleasure in the company of the humble, and occasionally had a meal or a drink at the café. A village woman, discussing him on her doorstep with a friend, saw our local coal merchant drive up in his lorry. Jumping down from the driving seat, the merchant proceeded to bring her a sack of coal.

'You're making a mistake,' said the woman. 'I didn't order any coal. I couldn't afford it.'

'I know,' said the coal merchant. 'That's why. It's a present from M. le Curé.'

A number of notables wrote to the bishop asking for another *curé*. The bishop, aware that an unpopular priest, however saintly, can be a danger to the Church, sent him to another parish. I recalled that short paragraph in one of my mother's letters: 'M. le Curé has left the village.' This had saddened me. It seemed out of tune with modern times.

The sea growled in the distance and there was a smell of seaweed. The beams of a lighthouse swept the bay of Le Havre. I climbed the hill and drove down my orchard. The house was asleep.

Matilda also was asleep, though I knew that in the morning she would tell me—and certainly believe it—that she had not closed her eyes all night and had heard me come in. Fifille did not bark and I went quietly up to bed. I turned on the radio and found some European station giving out the news. I began tidying up my room and putting out the dress I would wear in the morning. The wine from the Loire, like all white wines, would prevent me from sleeping but I didn't care. I slept far too much as it was. There was so much I wanted to read, so much I still wanted to learn.

An owl was hooting outside and I loved the sound. The bedside lamp and the heating made this bedroom in the middle of an orchard as comfortable as the one in Carring-ton House. But here the air was pure and the sounds of the night more thrilling. Always those lines of Horace would come back to mind. When one is in the town, one wants to be in the country; and when one is in the country, it is of the town that one thinks. Then suddenly for some reason I recalled a certain night in Paris. I had been to the theatre alone. The play was gay and charming, the actors young, the girls beautifully dressed. I decided to go home in the Métro, the way I had come. I hardly ever take a taxi. So I went down into the bowels of the earth, and to my utter surprise there seemed to be no passengers except myself, but the platform was full of sleeping figures; tramps in miserable clothes, coats torn at the elbow, gaping shoes showing dirty socks with holes. I had the impression of having walked into a novel by Gorky. These recumbent dark dregs of humanity appalled me, and I wondered how long I would have to wait for a train. I took my stand as near to the rails as I could. I could see the silvery gleam of the metal, the live rail running alongside the others. Suddenly a recumbent figure raised itself and addressed me. I was so terrified that I understood nothing. Then another sat up and his voice was added to that of the first. Then another. . . . They looked like dead men rising from their graves, and I began to look about me for a way of escape. From every side men shook themselves to a seated position and spoke. One might have supposed that they were demanding to know in what year, in what century, they were coming back to life. At last I understood. They were asking me the time.

'Was it midnight?' they asked.

To my shame, finding myself alone amongst this nocturnal population, I was afraid to look at my gold wrist-watch. I was terribly afraid, terribly afraid. I said I didn't know.

'Bourrique!' said the first who had asked me the question. 'She-ass!'

He lay down again. And the rest all in turn did the same. Then my train arrived and I flew into it. Later I understood that these *clochards* were turned out of the Métro when it closed, and that they wanted to know how much longer they could remain in the warmth.

The next day, when lunching with Marcel Haedrich and Juliette Gréco, I told them about my adventure and the terrible fear I had experienced, and how ashamed I was of it. How ashamed I was of having been afraid of the poor. Juliette Gréco looked at me with her big dark eyes and said: 'But poverty is always frightening . . . always . . . always.'

But in truth it is inequality that frightens, inequality in education, in fortune, in physical appearance.

The owl had stopped hooting and the house was very still. I had tidied everything up now, put all my things carefully away. I invariably began madly to turn round in circles, opening cupboards and shutting them, when I passed through various crises, when I was too excited to read, when my head was full of ideas, when memories started to choke me. For instance, why had my father, Milou, died when I was a child, before I was in a position to have given him the freedom of these orchards? My little house, my vegetable garden, my roses, would have given him such immense pleasure. Why was Matilda losing that insatiable interest she once had in life? Why was she dying?

She had got so little out of her brief passage. So many things tended to finish before they had really begun. I went softly down to look at her. She was still asleep. Her breathing was not the same as it used to be. There had been a change during the last few months.

She no longer undressed now but just lay down on her bed, her arms stretched out against her frail body. Every movement was torture. To raise her arms, to move her shoulders, to put on or to take off a woolly, was too much to expect of her. Why must she be tortured so? How unfortunate that at the very moment when I could at last give her material comforts I was helpless to alleviate her pain. One's powerlessness to give joy to a loved one is a bitter cross to bear.

I went back to bed and set my alarm clock for five o'clock. That was the hour for her first cortisone. The cock had already crowed. It was three o'clock. My cuckoo clock was broken. The little bird was stuck half way through the door, its beak pathetically open.

By morning the frost had disappeared but it was raining again, a fine persistent rain. I drove down to the village to get the bread, and noticed that the shopkeepers had all put their plants on the very edge of the pavement to drink in the rain. The butcher had put his aspidistra out, and I thought how nice it would be to own one. When I was a little girl we had one at Clichy and Matilda used to cover its soil with used coffee grounds, which were supposed to be good for it. When we came to live in London I saw that people used to put their used tea leaves on plants for the same reason. Now what does an aspidistra really like? Tea or coffee? I suppose it depends on which side of the Channel it is born. The same thing applies to superstitions. There is a great contradiction between the things that are supposed to be lucky and unlucky according to the country in which one lives. The family with whom I lodged when I first came to England omitted the street number of their house because it ought to have been a thirteen, and they considered that number unlucky. On the other hand I was born on a thirteenth, and everybody in Clichy considered it a good omen. English girls won't be married in May, whereas in France June is the month which brings tears:

> Le mois des fleurs
> Signe de pleurs.

We all agree that old wives' tales are nonsense, but I would hate to have a mind so serious and analytical that it would detach me from superstitions, portents and dreams.

On my return to the farm I took all my geraniums from the living-room, where they had passed the winter, and set them out on the flagstones in the garden. While they absorbed the beneficial rain, I looked about the room wondering how to change its aspect. Changing furniture is a woman's favourite occupation, and if men show less anxiety to employ their gifts in this direction it is probably because they spend fewer hours at home. My mother liked to tell the story of two spinster twins who lived in a tiny apartment at Blois, and who got so bored with each other's company that they spent hours trying to change the aspect of their living-room. They would push a heavy cupboard full of linen from one side of the room to the other. One day the cupboard toppled over on to one of the twins and fractured her hip. When her twin visited her in hospital she inquired about the apartment. Had she been changing the furniture about lately?

'No,' said the twin; 'now that I'm alone I don't make any more changes.'

The youth of Blois laughed a lot over this story, which now came back to me like so many of the stories my mother told me when I was a child. Perhaps now I understand the twins better. I plan changes in my house almost every day with a view to the future. A change invariably brings an improvement, even though it may prove short lived. Patsy, in whom I confided, exclaimed: 'I'm just the same. At winter sports this year I planned to redecorate my guest-room entirely. I could hardly wait to get home. I knew just what paper I wanted for the walls and I would cover the tables with flounces of gay chintz. I adore doing that sort of thing. I pictured the surprise and admiration of all my young friends when I ushered them into the guest-room transformed according to my dream. Well, what happened? My poor mother had her stroke and I had to put her in the guest-room. So the work never got done and I have to lodge my guests elsewhere or put them up at the inn.'

Three of my geranium cuttings were dead. The winter proved too long for them. Suddenly I had another idea. I would cut out a sleeveless blouse. Where are the scissors? Where is the material? I must get it finished before supper. Hurrah!

3

MY moments of happiness were brief. Always the shadow of my mother's suffering prevented me from enjoying the warmth of the sun, the song of the birds, the gnarled dignity of our apple trees. I lived half in the present, half in the past. 'Classically,' I called it when writing to my husband—'Corinne, the New Testament in Greek, Russian for Beginners, the dark earth, the kitchen—my sewing.' I added these words: 'I have just finished making a very pretty jumper, but now that my beauty is fading I would like to go to the university to fashion an interior beauty— a beauty of the mind. I love you infinitely and I can only hope that we are not wasting these days, separated from each other as we are—we who are growing old.'

My lonely nights were one long searching into the past, and the story of these terrible months would not be complete if I did not try to disembowel time and go backwards as well as forwards. Only thus can I get a clear picture of Matilda's martyrdom and my unhappy role as the daughter. Now it so happened that I was always putting my thoughts painfully on to paper, and while rummaging in my room one night I came upon some sheets, foolscap sheets written closely on both sides, which tell obliquely of some of the more poignant moments of our relationship. Three years must have elapsed since I wrote them. They belong to the time when I still rode up and down the hill on a bicycle, wasting the last vestiges of my strength—partly because I was so afraid to spend money and partly because I was so convinced that I was too incompetent to drive a car. Self-assurance is what I have most lacked. Could I have given more to Matilda if it had not been for this defect?

These pages attack the subject by a circuitous route. I can never go straight to the point. My nature is to go round and round as if I were afraid to show my hand. So my story begins with a visit to Jacques Déliquaire's farm, the one we call Berlequet.

There was nobody at home when I arrived to fetch the milk. The German tractor was not in the garage. Only Wallis, the farm dog, barked at my approach and then wagged its tail because it knew me. Georgette had left the milk can hanging from the buttery door. I unhooked it and, followed by Wallis and Fifille, decided to inspect my farmer's kitchen garden.

To walk into a neighbour's garden in his absence is almost like penetrating into his home. I felt a little guilty, but when I reached the potato patch I came upon a man digging. Though I had never seen him before, I made as if I had expected to find him there and held out my hand, bidding him good day. We spend a great deal of time shaking hands in Normandy. He looked up, took the proffered hand and returned the salutation.

The palm of his hand was as hard as pumice-stone and yet this gardener, who was obviously hiring himself out by the day, was extremely young. Gardeners when you could find them, which was not often, were generally over sixty and retired. There were three old men who lived along the road to St Vaast who sometimes condescended to do a little work for me, but they all had pensions from the State, which would have represented quite a large capital if they had been obliged as in the old days to put money aside for their old age, and they didn't really want to earn any more. When one of them did come it was mostly to drink my cider and talk about their youth—the days when they were in the army and soldiers wore red trousers, looked after horses and were paid in gold. I had heard it all before and my garden made no progress.

'So you're a gardener?' I said, proclaiming the obvious.

'Yes, madame.'

'Could you work for me at all?'

'I could,' he said, 'but I'm really looking for regular work. I come from Alençon and I'm new here.'

We agreed a price and he promised to come the next morning at seven for a twelve-hour day. On my return home I said to Matilda: 'I've found a gardener, a young man with a long nose who just now is digging Jacques's potato patch. He comes from Alençon.' I thought this might interest her because she had spent so much of her young married life making up lace blouses and, as she knew better than anybody, Alençon lace is amongst the finest of the fine. My mother didn't answer right away and my thoughts wandered. I began to remember a journey my husband and I made to Biarritz when we were newly married. It suddenly struck me that I had been very young once, gay and irresponsible. I must not forget that. I must not allow contact with my ailing mother to make me feel old. So as I went up to my room I thought back with pleasure to that journey which we made in a clover leaf Citroën bought second hand for twenty pounds. We were very young journalists and not at all afraid impudently to park our car next to the Hispano-Suizas, Rolls-Royces and Bentleys in front of the Chambre d'Amour in this most fashionable of all resorts. Because of her capricious nature we thought of this fantastic vehicle as being of the feminine gender and called her Totote. Sometimes we left her outside the Hôtel du Palais and during the aperitif hour we would leave her outside the Bar Basque while we tried, with the help of olives and potato chips, to make our rose cocktail last long enough for us to note the doings of the smart set who bowed and curtsied to King

Alfonso of Spain and Edward, Prince of Wales, who at that time was everybody's darling. When the bar, which was in the open air, emptied itself, we lunched cheaply on figs and melons.

Youth in itself does not make one happy. Alas, I was unhappy at Biarritz. We skirted the luxury of this extremely expensive town, not being rich enough to plunge unheedingly into its gay life, and I was at the age when a girl's pleasures count for a lot. A girl in her early twenties does not stop to think. Each hour is too vividly precious. I wanted to dance, to see, to be seen, to wear beautiful dresses and go where the smart people went. I would need more years before discovering how to manufacture my own happiness. This was in part due to the fact that with my marriage I was beginning a second slice of life. My youth, the years of my childhood, had been too dramatically hard. My only thought was to forget the black bread. Not for some years did those early days come surging up again, choking me, insisting that I should finally get rid of them by long hours of exhausting, enchanting, tearful work writing *The Little Madeleine*.

Robert, Totote and I, conscious of our poverty, sweltering in the heat, made an excursion into Spain, where I rediscovered some peace of mind, for Totote could now nod in a friendly way to carts drawn by oxen, carts with solid wooden wheels. It was on the way home from that journey that we visited Alençon.

There was not only the lace. In the days of my mother's youth, before the 1914 war, there was amongst such famous *demi-mondaines* as La Belle Otéro, Cléo de Mérode, Diane de Pougy, one Émilienne d'Alençon. I had heard Matilda discussing her with friends at Clichy, for I was a silent party to all her conversations and I was a very wide-awake little girl. But I had another reason to be interested in this beauty and the place of her birth. Before embarking on this Biarritz holiday I had engaged at our flat in Brompton Road a morning help by the name of Mme Bathilde, who, if I remember rightly, came to us through an advertisement in Soho.

'Ah,' said Mme Bathilde, shelling peas, which was one of her favourite occupations, 'when I was a young dressmaker in Paris we used to work for Émilienne d'Alençon. Her underskirts had so many flounces that we would run a fever making them up, but all the gentlemen in Paris were mad about her and she was to be seen everywhere. When she went to the races there would be photographs of her in the papers, and we would cut them out and pin them up above our sewing-machines next to one of Sarah Bernhardt. We not only heard of her adventures by reading the papers but from her maid, whom we got to know when we went to the house to deliver a dress. Mademoiselle, as we called the maid, was always happy to talk about Madame. She would treat us well because she ended by having nearly all Madame's dresses. Madame would not dare to give them to anybody else. Once, when Mademoiselle in my presence undid the box containing a new dress we had made for Madame, she exclaimed: "Oh, that colour doesn't suit me at all. I shall have to persuade her not to have another like it." On another occasion she said: "You make Madame's dresses, but I persuade her which one to wear. Of course there is the imponderable. If her evening is successful the dress she wore will become a favourite and it will be a long time before I can get hold of it; if, on the other hand, the evening proves a failure, she will come home in a temper, tear off the dress and stamp on it. That's where I benefit." Mme Bathilde was superb when re-enacting these scenes and the peas would fly through her fingers. She would go on: 'Then, Mme Henrey, there were the days when we had to wait for Madame. Sometimes Mademoiselle would beguile us by taking us into her bedroom. I was twenty at that time. Oh, Madame's bedroom! It was unbelievable. Carpets of panther skins with their heads and savage teeth. High muslin curtains that looked like clouds which might have fallen from the sky. They stretched from ceiling to floor. And Madame's bed! With a tester like at Versailles. And all those mirrors and perfumes! "Everything is in white just now," Mademoiselle would point out. "All ready for this evening when Madame will come back with Monsieur from the Jockey Club. But perhaps after dinner she will want a change, and then we shall change all the curtains, the draperies and the bedcover. And everything will be pink. Or perhaps blue. Even the sheets. That's what the word luxury means, my girl!"'

This then, as well as the lace, was why I wanted to visit Alençon.

Had Émilienne once been a goose girl at Alençon? From what humble origin had she sprung? What had made her take the name of this city? After lunch I insisted that my husband should find a place where we could inspect some Alençon lace. When the Huguenot lace-makers of Alençon fled to Honiton did they not bring new glory to England with the superb Point d'Angleterre? A M. Lefébure, we were told, kept some fine pieces under glass. We hurried to his shop and even saw some made by Sainte Thérèse de Lisieux. They were of such beauty that they seemed to me sufficient reason in itself to admit her to heaven.

'I wouldn't count on your new gardener coming to-morrow,' said Matilda at dinner.

Why did she want to break my joy? There were moments like this when what she said chilled me. Did she want to hurt or was it merely that she was protecting herself against hope? We were in the kitchen with the garden door wide open, and I was wondering how to answer her dutifully when the stillness of the evening was broken by piercing bird cries. Celestina, our black cat, was carrying a fledgling in her jaws, and the mother bird, perched on a plum tree, was making demented noises. I sprang up, released the tiny thing from between the cat's sharp, cruel teeth and brought it tenderly into the kitchen. Its heart, as I held it against my breast, was still beating, but could I save it? I turned hopefully to Matilda; but in a voice charged with years and experience she said: 'You haven't a hope—not when they are as young as that.' But my fledgling, as if it understood her, opened a large bright eye—an eye that seemed almost too big for its tiny head. Cradled in my cupped hands it weighed nothing at all. After a while it seemed to revive in the warmth of my hands and this time Matilda said: 'You should put it in a hedge high enough for the cats not to get at it.' Followed by Fifille I set off across the orchard. The tall pear tree was bending in the wind and rain was starting to fall. I had not the heart to abandon my fledgling to the cats, the wind and the rain so I brought it back to the house, put it in a very small basket and brought it up to my bedroom. I listened to Big Ben, the news and a play, and soon fell asleep. The next morning I expected to find my patient dead, but when I uncovered the basket he was very much alive and flew against a mirror. After some trouble I caught him and took him to the open window, through which he flew without a backward look.

Matilda at the kitchen door called: 'Your gardener is here!' I dressed quickly and went down to welcome him. I led him to the kitchen garden, and while we worked he told me more about himself.

'My name is Bricotte,' he said. 'Yes, it's a funny name— Jacques Bricotte—and I'm twenty-eight. My wife is called Simone and our daughter Giselle. My wife was furious not to have a boy. Women always seem to want boys. If I'd have owned something, a piece of land, for instance, I would have been glad to have a son, but as I own nothing a girl is better.

'My parents had a small hotel at Alençon, but I suppose I got in their way, for they sent me to boarding school. I was about eleven when the Allies invaded France. The hotel was destroyed during a bombing raid, my parents with it. Nobody told me, so that when term came to an end I was looking forward to going home. I was turned over to the Assistance Publique. You know what that means. People are not particularly kind to foundlings. In many ways they are still treated as they were a hundred years ago. I was sent to work on a farm. We had to plant potatoes, dig them up, put them into sacks. All the odd jobs fell to us. One day I was told to churn the milk, but I was too small to turn the handle. The farmer was so angry that he rubbed a fistful of nettles against my cheeks till they burned. He thought I was just idling. He said that a good nettle rash would keep me on the hop. I tried to free myself by putting down my name for Indo-China. I thought I could kill, get my revenge, give as many kicks as I had received. Meanwhile I got work with a demolition squad, mostly Poles and Italians, who quarrelled and fought all day. One man, however, hept to himself during the dinner break. He would go off into a corner and heat his food over a fire of twigs and dead wood. I could hardly believe it when he asked me to share his meal. It was the first time that anybody had ever done me a kindness. I didn't even know how to thank him. I hadn't been taught. One Sunday he took me home to meet his wife. She found a little corner for me, a comfortable bed, clean sheets. I ended by staying with them. The second phase of my life had begun.'

The morning was far advanced. Jacques Déliquaire arrived with his tractor to tidy up a pile of wood. Bricotte went to help him. The two men were now perched on the high seat. Their young voices carried across the orchard.

There is nothing more agreeable for a woman than to have men working round her. She feels she is protected.

On returning to the house I found Matilda in the throes of a monstrous attack. My happiness melted away and I felt sick with disappointment. Lately she had seemed so much better. Her wonderful appetite had come back, and she was cooking again some of those delightful dishes which had rightly given her the reputation of being *un cordon bleu*. She had even helped me sow some corn on the cob in the big garden. We had been on the verge of recapturing our lovely mother-daughter relationship. Once I caught her laughing and it seemed to flood the orchard in warm sunshine. She might have been twenty again. Now I should wander like a ghost through the saddened house, fearing to make a noise.

At five o'clock I took my bicycle and went down to the village in the hope of finding her something tempting for supper. The wind blew through my hair and whipped my cheeks as I sped down the steep hill. The village was very gay. How I envied these young mothers pushing their babies in a pram. Is there anything more wonderful for a young woman than to be able to give pleasure to others! The baby in the pram sees the blue sky sailing along above him like a ribbon. His eyes look with wonderment at the changing scenes.

But except for those occasional excursions into the kitchen garden which would presumably stop now, my mother remained motionless as a waxen figure at the corner of the kitchen table. When I brought anybody into the house and we happened to talk about a friend's villa, or what had happened on the *plage*, or if we even mentioned the honeysuckle and dog roses that garlanded the country lanes, she would assume the look of a prisoner who is prevented by steel bars and cruel wardens from leaving her cell.

'If only I had the moral courage!' I cried. 'If only I had as much courage as every other woman has—to buy and drive

a little car! Then I could make the corner of that table fly
over hill and dale. I could help my mother to escape that
daily boredom and come with me into towns and cities
from which she has been barred for so long.'

On leaving the chemist's, where I ordered great new doses
of cortisone, I met Hélène Vincent.

'I'm so happy!' she cried. 'Jean and I have just got
delivery of our new car. Now we must find somebody to
buy our old one.'

'Heaven has made you cross my path,' I said. 'I'll buy
your old car.'

'Very well,' said Hélène. 'I'll tell Jean.'

Jean telephoned me that evening. I feared when I heard
his voice that he was going to tell me that he had already dis-
posed of his car. Those two-horse-power Citroëns were very
cheap to run and at that time were in short supply. All he
said was: 'Do you still want to buy my old car? Because I
shall be delighted to sell it to you. I'm going to an auction
in the country tomorrow, but why not come down on
Friday and try it. Then if you like it you can drive it straight
back to the farm.'

Friday has always been my lucky day. When as a girl I
worked as a manicurist at London's Savoy the English girls
were always warning me about the things one must not do
on a Friday, such as turning one's mattress, wearing a new
dress or a new pair of shoes, putting a clean handkerchief
into one's handbag. These things all spelt disaster. But in
fact though I did not tempt providence I generally did very
well on a Friday. Occasionally I made more in tips that day
than during all the rest of the week.

So on Friday I called at the notary's office, where Jean was
waiting for me. We drove in the direction of Blonville and
on the whole I did rather well. My husband had given me
innumerable lessons in London, and I even owned a
British driving licence that dated from the time when there

were no driving tests. But I had always had my husband beside me, or nearly always, so that it didn't really matter if I did anything wrong. Jean was pleasantly surprised to see how well I managed. He had been afraid that his wife was going to make him teach me to drive in order to effect the sale. He merely said that women were stupid creatures who thought that everything their husbands did could be done just as easily by themselves, whereas of course what men did so well was the result of years and years of experience.

To put his mind at rest I told him I would buy the car—in fact that he could consider it already sold. The formalities took no time at all. We called at the town hall and at the post office, and as his father's clerk was the local insurance agent we took out a policy immediately. From that moment the car was mine. I would get the official papers on Monday. But we decided that I would not drive it home before lunch. I would ride my bicycle home and Jean would bring me the car at about two o'clock.

One did not, of course, ride a bicycle up the hill which was far too steep. One flew down it and one pushed the bicycle up it. I hoped sincerely that this would be the last time in my life that I would ever have to accomplish this laborious act. Ever since the war I had brought up all my provisions from the village in this way, like the poorest of the poor, and it had worn me out. There are times when one can push the art of saving money too far. I had begun to hate myself.

At the agreed hour, looking over my garden fence, I saw the motorized cavalcade bumping over the rough tufts of grass. Jean was driving my car; Hélène was driving theirs. I did a few turns round the apple trees. Then Hélène and Jean drove away and I was almost surprised to see the grey vehicle they had left behind—my 'pram'.

Matilda was sceptic. I could have expected that. Before committing herself she needed proof.

'I've been let down too often,' she said. 'I don't enthuse easily.'

I sympathized with her, but she may not have realized how uninspiring it was for others. I needed encouragement dreadfully.

'I'm afraid of everything,' Matilda went on. 'When I'm in pain I'm afraid. When the pain leaves me I'm afraid of it coming back worse than it was before. If I won a sweepstake I wouldn't believe it unless I saw the money piled up in front of me on the kitchen table. Even then I'd be afraid they had made a mistake.'

When Matilda had gone back into the kitchen I did some more rodeo round the apple trees, but the engine kept on stalling, and when I switched it on again it made an appalling noise. I was grateful that the cows were not in the orchard. I felt ashamed.

Matilda, reading *Dr Zhivago*, showed no interest in my manœuvres. I could see the top of her golden hair at the far end of the table. I felt abandoned. And to think it was for her that I had taken this dramatic step. But when at last I parked my 'pram' by the garden gate, she greeted me with the words: 'Well, at least you can make it go. I'll put the kettle on.'

I began to read the book of instructions that Jean had left me but everything got confused and I decided to think no more about it till the morning. I took a knife and went to cut a lettuce in the kitchen garden, but more than half of them had been massacred by our chickens who were always flying over the white barrier. We had such trouble to grow the vegetables, and then all these chickens that I kept merely to amuse Matilda destroyed them. I went back to get scissors to cut their wings. The next thing was to catch them. I dipped a piece of bread in warm milk, put it under a sieve which I propped up with a stick to which I attached a long string. After catching two and losing all my bread, the others made off across the orchard. I could have wept. Everything was such hard work and I had nobody to turn to. If only Robert were with me I could have cried on his shoulder. He would have comforted me.

Returning to the front of the house I caught sight of my 'pram'. Supposing that by tomorrow I had quite forgotten how to drive it? Could such a thing happen? Or was it like a bicycle—once learnt, never forgotten? I got into the driving seat, switched on the engine and drove up to the main gate, which I opened and passed through. Now I was in the lane on the way to Montauzan. Here indeed was Montauzan with its gleaming white pillars. I had done everything so secretly that even Patsy didn't know about my acquisition. Just now, however, I was so afraid of bumping into her gates that I went straight down the hill to the village, past the police station, past the notary's house, into the main street. Here was the post office. Circumventing the roundabout I reached our baker's shop and, though I had no money on me, I bought a freshly baked loaf a yard long which I put on the seat beside me. There was rather a steep gradient and I no sooner released the hand brake than my car began to run backwards. I put the brake on again and felt a wind of panic. What must I do? The bakeress ran down the steps of her shop, opened the car door and deftly put me into gear. 'There, Mme Henrey,' she said. 'Try again.'

I drove back to the farm and put the warm bread on the kitchen table. Matilda looked up from *Dr Zhivago*. I thought I saw a tiny glint of admiration in her eyes. Could it be that she was getting interested? I felt like a girl who has got to the top of her class.

Because Matilda was nearly always in it, the kitchen was never quite mine. If I tried to bake a cake or make jam I knew that she would be watching me from her chair at the corner of the table, and I was so certain that she was silently criticizing me that I would fluff everything and then lose my temper. It was the same if I tried to make a dress or a blouse. I was still in her eyes the child who must be made to unpick the wrong stitches.

So except when I had to iron I left the kitchen to her. She made incredible stews for her cats which remained for hours at a time on the slow plate of the Aga, giving forth a strange aroma. The cats loved her passionately, which was natural, and they arched their backs against her poor legs as she shuffled from the kitchen to her own room and back from her room into the kitchen.

My bedroom, on the other hand, was my delight. I could turn the radio on as loud as I liked and switch from station to station—German, English or French. The birds made a wonderful noise in the branches of the cherry tree, devouring the fruit before it ripened and long before I got a chance to pick it. The tits came to my window for the coconut and the bread. Fifille would ask to be put on the bed, and then go fast asleep with her head between her paws. Her breathing was like a well-regulated motor. She gave me the illusion that I was not alone.

Patsy and her mother had been brightening several of the rooms at Montauzan. They had been buying yards of flowered cotton, for instance, to run up as curtains. Patsy's nicest idea was to give her daughter Anne a room of her own and to do it up for her in the loveliest way in pink with a bed just the right size, small tables and shelves on the walls. When I was first invited to inspect it, the sun was shining, and the big french windows which were thrown open gave one the impression of being half in the garden. A kitten was curled up asleep in the little girl's osier armchair. Her brother Pascal also had his own room. This was decorated in orange, with curtains of sail cloth bought during a holiday in Marseilles. Pascal had arranged his treasures to form a little museum. Every piece had a label giving its origin, a pebble, for instance, which his parents had brought back from Athens, a rabbit's paw. The spelling was so strange that I laughed.

'I wanted to correct him,' said Patsy, 'but that would have taken all our fun away.'

Matilda's sewing-machine was now so old and cumbersome that I dreamed of owning a really modern one. What a splendid summer it would be if in addition to my car I could have one of those electric machines that could do even the most complicated stitches! Perhaps the fact that I was separated by the broad width of the channel from my husband was making me want to assert my personality. I had been curbing my desires for so long.

At this juncture Patsy asked me to come with her to Caen where she wanted to buy more furnishing materials. She also needed some white rep to make herself a pair of skin-tight slacks. The ones she had made earlier in the season had been a great success, but when she washed them they shrunk so much that she couldn't get into them again.

'Of course they won't be wasted', she explained, 'because they will do for Anne, but this time I shall take care to wash the material before I start to cut it.' She added as a sort of challenge: 'A good sewing-machine does encourage one to make clothes.'

That decided me. 'I thought of buying a really modern one,' I said. 'It would probably cost me as much as the car, but I feel I've suddenly grown up. Those Swiss and Italian models are almost human.'

Patsy was not the sort of person to put me off a whim. She drove me to a shop in the Rue de l'Écuyère where a very pretty girl in a white overall, which made her look like an *esthéticienne* in a beauty parlour, showed us what she called the pearl of her collection, a Bernina, which at the gentlest touch could do almost everything, even embroidering with two different needles in two different colours.

'Miraculous!' said Patsy. 'And of course you can make zigzags,' said the girl, 'which are marvellously useful if you want to make yourself a girdle.'

Patsy did the negotiating. The machine would be delivered not to my farm, which nobody could be expected to find, but to Montauzan, which was a real house with a drive. Patsy would call me on the phone. I would then hurry to her place and we would all have another lesson.

David Owen was to come to tea the following afternoon. He was going to bring me back a saw that I had lent him and I would bake some scones and a cake. I would also produce bread and butter and strawberry jam (made by Granny) —a real English tea.

I had just taken the scones out of the oven when Fifille started to bark. The girl from Caen, accompanied by a woman who might well have been her mother, was arriving with the Bernina.

'We couldn't find Montauzan,' said the girl. 'I don't think we would have found you either if it hadn't been for a man who was cutting grass in a ditch by the side of the lane. He told us to go on till we came to a fork. "You can't miss it," said the little man. "The least good lane is the right one. It's not good but it's right. See?"'

'I've seen him before,' I explained. 'The other day he was fast asleep on a bed of nettles, his scythe beside him. Two young people passing in a car (they were certainly not from this part of the world) braked suddenly when they saw him and got out, thinking he was either ill or dead. His face was buried in the crook of his arm to protect him from the hot sun. The strangers shook him gently: "Are you all right?" one of them asked. As there was no answer they

shook him again more vigorously. At last he stirred, tried to
return to the waking world, and finally told them to be off
and leave him in peace and get the hell out of it. The poor
innocents stepped back as if they had seen the devil and,
getting back into their car, drove off at top speed.'

'In that case,' said the girl, 'we were fortunate to find
him on his two feet!'

Now David came swinging down the orchard with my
cross-cut saw, his black shoes well shined as befitted an old
soldier. The Bernina was arranged on a table in the low
room so that I could be given another demonstration. I
asked the elder woman if she was the girl's mother.

'No,' she answered. 'She's my demonstrator. My name is
Mme Chanu and my husband owns the shop. You doubtless
saw him when you came in yesterday with your friend.'

I had indeed noticed a man wearing an overall and a blue
beret. I spent the next few minutes watching the demonstrator put the complicated machine through its paces.
Matilda was talking to David in the kitchen, but as her
command of English was not what it used to be she shouted
at him at the top of her little girl's voice, and he for some
reason shouted back. She was in the throes of yet another
crisis and could hardly drag herself round the kitchen table,
but she insisted on making the tea herself, brewing it in the
biggest teapot in the house. Cutting short my sewing lesson
I laid the table, cut the bread and butter and put out the cake
and the warm scones. Our friends from Caen were surprised,
I think, to find themselves invited to such an English
meal.

The demonstrator told us that she was from Rouen and
was twenty-four. She had passed her driving test some
months earlier in order to go more easily round the countryside visiting customers, many of whom were young women
anxious to keep up with the newest ideas. Her make-up
and fashionable hair-do contrasted with Mme Chanu's black

ensemble. Even the scarf and stockings were black. I inquired if she was in mourning.

'I am,' she answered, 'and I shall never leave it. Two years ago I lost my only son. He went off on his bicycle one day and was wedged against the kerb by a lorry, which knocked him down and ran over him. He died four hours later in hospital. For my husband and me it was the end of everything. We had implored him to buy a scooter. We felt that a scooter would be safer. But he said: "It's easier to thread one's way through the traffic with a bicycle and I'm so used to it." He was married. His wife was expecting her second baby, but as she was from Algeria she decided after his death to go back to her family with her child. So she went back and had her second child there. One cannot blame her, but my husband and I lost almost overnight our son, our daughter-in-law and our grandchildren. And as our home had been reduced to rubble during the invasion, I didn't even have a picture of my son when he was little, nor any of his childhood toys, to remember him by. He was just wiped off the face of the earth, and soon I shall find it hard to remember what he looked like.'

Her story cast a new sadness over the house. Selfishly it struck me that I might have been wiser than I guessed to buy Jean's little car.

When next day I tried to use my new sewing-machine I found that I had forgotten all the instructions. I spent more than an hour studying the book and turning tiny wheels this way and that, but the more I tried the less I understood. Matilda, to whom I ran for consolation, said ironically: 'You ought to have bought another baby Singer like the one you have in London. It would have cost you a quarter of the price and at least you would have had no difficulty in making it work.'

Her good sense made me feel worse, and yet something inside me insisted that I had been right to let myself go. I found myself thinking: Matilda is sarcastic by nature. She has always relied on her hands, her feet and her capacity for hard work to pull her through. Now they have let her down. She worked too hard. She wore herself out. One doesn't have to do that any longer.

For two days I lived through a nightmare during which everything I tried to do went wrong. When I put my car into reverse I would bump into an apple tree. When I made a new effort to understand my Bernina, the needle stuck or the cotton got snarled up, and I ended by thinking I had broken a vital part. Instead of advancing in life I was going backwards. I was useless. I couldn't even please my mother. Whenever I tried to say something nice to her she answered ironically. I went up to my bedroom and lay dejectedly on my bed. Fifille licked my face. I thought of a song that my grandmother had crooned over me when I was a little girl at Blois—about a little boy who was always too small to become something or somebody. He was not tall enough to be in the bodyguard of Louis XVI, *dame voui*, went the song; he was too small to shoe a horse, *dame voui*; he was so small that he got himself killed by a cannon ball, *dame voui*; and when he arrived in heaven St Peter said to him: 'You're far too little, my friend, *dame voui*; to come in here, *dame voui*':

> Tu es bien trop petit, mon ami, dame voui,
> Pour entrer ici, dame voui.

But at that moment Jesus came along and drew little Gregory into the protection of His rose-coloured cloak, saying gently:

> 'Mon ciel de gloire
> C'est pour les petits,
> Mon ami, dame voui.'

My grandmother's voice was cracked but she made me cry—and be happy too. It helped me to believe—and never to give up hope, not even when one was as small and stupid as I was. Did not Bergson say: 'We live to strive'?

I did not fall asleep till I heard the first birds at dawn. First one at a great distance, then others nearer. I had set my alarm clock for half past six and, slipping on a dressing-gown, went to open the stable door and to give the chickens their first meal. This was the moment of the day that invariably made up for all my disappointments. The country air smelt so sweet. The cats had come into the kitchen after hunting all night, and were perched like sphinxes on the Aga, their eyes glued to the handle of my mother's door.

'I shall go to Caen,' I exclaimed suddenly. 'I shall insist on being taught all the intricacies of my Bernina. How is it that at my age I still hesitate to demand what is my due? Why am I so afraid to importunate people?'

I went up and dressed. I gathered up my papers and a toy bear which I had given to my son when he was little and which the moths were now getting at.

'You also, Fifille,' I said, 'will be my companion, for you don't laugh at my mistakes. You trust me implicitly. You think that everything I do is for the best.'

A few minutes later I had passed through the gate and was on my way to Caen.

The magnificently rebuilt city seemed effervescent. A fair had brought in visitors from all round. The traffic seemed to be composed either of tiny cars like mine or trucks as large as houses. After a moment or two I got my bearing, and my joy at finding myself in full view of M. Chanu's establishment was such that I parked my car in front of the porte cochère of a small printing works. In addition I was wedged against another car. Fortunately a young apprentice, seeing my plight, came to my rescue, and helped me push the car very neatly in front of the shop, so that all was well except that I was still a bit flushed and everybody would know that I lacked experience as a driver. The young demonstrator in her white overall was looking cool and efficient, and when I informed her of the reason of my visit I thought I could detect the slightest change in her manner as if she were thinking—as indeed I might have done in her place—that as she had already sold me the Bernina any further talks between us could only degenerate into a waste of time. Perhaps I was over-sensitive, but did her rapid technical explanations hide a suspicion of contempt? Poor woman, I imagined her thinking, she has a car which she doesn't even know how to park neatly against the kerb and an expensive sewing-machine which she can't work. That's the sort of person who has money these days whereas I have the thankless task of, etc. etc.

'Mademoiselle,' I said severely, 'I am not going to leave this shop until I have mastered every detail of this wonderful machine. So let's get down to work.'

She appeared momentarily taken aback. For all I know she may have been full of good intentions and I may have entirely misjudged her. But I took a pencil and a piece of paper and wrote down her instructions in shorthand. When she had finished I read back what I had written and put it into practice. This time I had understood.

'I bid you good day, Mademoiselle,' I said, and walked out of the shop.

My return journey passed without incident, and as soon as I was back at the farm I hurried up to my room to make sure that I had forgotten nothing. I spent the next five minutes successfully embroidering a yellow duster. Matilda came to the bottom of the stairs to say that lunch was ready. She had made me one of her specialities—*tomates farcies*. The sun was hot and I felt more at peace with the world, though it would have been nice if my mother could have shown greater interest in my exploit. Did she realize what it meant to drive to Caen and back all alone? Fortunately Patsy telephoned.

'Your mother told me you had gone,' she said. 'I could
hardly believe it. How brave you are!'

How pleasant it is to feel admired!

'I was terrified,' I said. 'Terrified. But you should see the
duster I've just embroidered. I can work it perfectly now.'

The Bernina sat on the table in my bedroom under the
window through which one had that lovely view of the
Louis XIII château. Patsy was just as excited about my new
toy as I was. She would say: 'Can I come and do something
important on your wonderful sewing-machine?' And I
would feel suitably flattered.

She was making Anne a tiny petticoat for her fifth birthday, and she had come to do the flounces on the Bernina.
Anne was playing with the moth-eaten bear I had taken as a
mascot to Caen. A feeling of contentment filled my bedroom. At a touch of a wheel the Bernina turned out em-
broidery that it would have taken months for the women in
a *béguinage* to accomplish by hand. It lacked the magnificence
of the hand-made thing, of course, but it was surprising,
useful and very even. We mounted the flounces to the petticoat with a zigzag stitch. The machine purred deliciously.

Small joys such as these were only like a curtain-raiser to
what was filling my mind with excitement and apprehension
—my first drives with Matilda. Would they be for her the
joy and wonderment I hoped?

For once I was not disappointed. We went for a drive
almost every evening. My mother quickly discovered the
easiest, by which I mean the least painful, way to slip into
the seat beside me, and then off we would go with Fifille
curled up on her lap.

We were fortunate, of course, in having some of the most

beautiful and romantic country in the whole of France all about us. Unless we wanted to go along the sea coast to Trouville or Deauville there was no need even to cross a highway. We could criss-cross the entire Pays d'Auge along peaceful unfrequented lanes where the tall tree-lined hedges were garlanded with honeysuckle and wild roses, where wood-strawberries clung to the ditches, and where in early spring the air was sweet with the smell of violets, primroses and wild narcissi. In autumn also I know no part of the country where blackberries and hazel-nuts are more abundant. And in every orchard farmers would be beating down the ripe cider apples which they stacked in golden heaps at the foot of the trees.

But we were in summer and in the hedges the wild cherry trees were black with ripe fruit. Matilda would say to me: 'This evening let's go to Annebault.' And sometimes when I was afraid of having taken a wrong lane, a wrong tunnel of green, she would say, 'No, we're on the right road. I recognize that tree', or occasionally she would be even more precise, exclaiming: 'There is that branch that overhangs the road. I noticed it only yesterday.' Her attention to detail was immense. She must have examined the hedges as we drove past them (oh, not very fast!) as in her youth she looked with admiration at every stitch in a piece of old lace. This surely was enough to show me that though she might not know how to express herself she was grateful for this new window on the world.

I made a thousand driving mistakes. I blush now at what must have been crass stupidity, for I was the sort of woman driver who exemplified the irresponsible minority in our sex. But I had the immense advantage of carrying two passengers, my mother and Fifille, who, knowing nothing about mechanics or the art of driving, were convinced that whatever I did was well done. They showed a touching faith in my capacity.

The route to Annebault is particularly fine, but at one point it crossed the new road they were building to connect the great bridge at Tancarville with the city of Caen, and a great yellow notice said: 'DEVIATION—CHANTIER.' In a moment of panic or aberration I penetrated the forbidden road-work, whereupon all the workmen, incited by the *patronne* of the local cabaret, her red hands resting determinately on her hips, barred my passage. Their invectives froze me up. I would reverse five yards and then lurch back into my rocky prison of broken stone. My impotence and the knowledge that these people had right on their side brought on my tears. The *patronne* softened.

'Hard over to the left!' she exhorted. Then after a moment: 'No, my good lady, not to the right!'

Her husband detached himself from the group to come and help me. He was patient and gentle and soon put me back on the road.

'If only you had come to help me right away, instead of frightening me!' I said to the man. 'Don't *you* ever make a mistake?'

'Doesn't *he* ever make a mistake!' cried his wife, 'But he does nothing else! *Allez, ma petite dame.* Off you go and have a nice drive.'

So along the lanes again till we came to Annebault.

The village with its poetic name and medieval church had been the home of Old Hommet, who played such a terrible role in the drama that brought murder to my farm during the German occupation. It was here, after inciting his small grandson to sell his father to the Gestapo for money, that the odious old sorcerer at the moment of his arrest took advantage of a moment's inattention on the part of the *gendarmes* to cut his throat. We now looked for the house where he and his wife had lived, but either it had disappeared or I had forgotten its exact location.

We went back home by a different set of lanes. While

peering into the leafy hedges from her comfortable seat beside me, Matilda enumerated the various menus which she had in mind for the coming week. As for this evening, she said, she had made a bread-and-butter pudding, which by now would be turning golden in the Aga. Georgette had brought her some cream from the farm. That was something to look forward to. I turned quickly to look at her. For the first time for many years she gave the impression of being happy, and it struck me that I, her daughter, could claim some of the credit for this. I felt rather like a husband who goes to work for the pleasure of earning enough money to spoil his family.

Ahead of us in this lane, whose tall leafy trees made an arch above the car, walked a young woman wearing jeans and Wellingtons, and leading a donkey on a long rope. On either side of the saddle were heavy milk cans. This little procession took up all the middle of the lane, and I was full of wonder at this blending of old and new. The young woman, hearing the noise of my car, looked over her shoulder. Her features, without a trace of make-up, her long slim neck and the vigorous auburn hair which framed her face, gave her the sort of natural beauty that one associates with tales of long ago. She would only have needed to change into a dress to meet the prince at the castle ball. She touched her donkey on its flank and it moved into the side of the lane, remaining motionless under the boughs of an over-spreading oak tree. I thanked the girl as I passed. I always have an uncomfortable feeling, when having to hustle a donkey to the side of the road, or cattle, or geese, that I am showing bad manners. In a sense it is so much more their road than ours.

There were evenings also when I would drive Matilda down to the sea. She would stay in the car with some binoculars my husband had given me and examine the little ships a mile or two out, or again, she would try to discover new points of interest all along the distant side of the bay, or gaze at Le Havre with its busy harbour and great refineries. She would try to imagine what it would be like to live in those modern blocks of flats which had lately been going up all along the waterfront.

On these occasions I would take Fifille and run barefoot along the sands. At this hour there were few people—sometimes an old women with a garden rake searching the damp sands for various kinds of bivalve shellfish like clams. Along our part of the coast they are known as *fillons*. The connoisseurs make *omelettes-aux-fillons*, which they eat with a glass of Muscadet, but both the gathering of them and their preparation require infinite patience. At other times a little boat would come in with a catch of plaice and mackerel, and for a few francs we could bring some home for supper.

So the days went by and I was beginning to feel that I was at last giving a few moments of pleasure to Matilda. There was no improvement in her condition. Indeed she was taking ever-increasing doses of cortisone, but it allowed her to go on moving painfully about the kitchen and occasionally making a few pots of jam. She insisted also on helping me with the fowls.

We had a magnificent cock in the farmyard who was ferociously pecking the hens, whose backs were beginning to bleed. Feeling sorry for these young ladies I had decided to catch this powerful male and eat him. We had too many cocks anyway, and I was paying out such large sums for grain that it was high time that I got some return, besides eggs, for my money.

I had more or less finished plucking the bird by lunch time. We spent the meal discussing where to go in the evening. The more interest Matilda showed in her drives the greater was my reward. She was beginning to know every small, picturesque village for twenty miles round, and her sense of direction was even better than mine. We thus had a safe subject of conversation.

After I had trussed the bird Matilda asked me to pour her some methylated spirit into a saucer so that she could singe it. She struck a match, and while I went to put the bottle away held the bird over the blue flame. The fowl must have been heavier than she expected, or else she really had no strength left at all in those poor knotted fingers, though I suspect that she was holding it between the palms of her hands, or even between her wrists. I never liked to look too closely how she did things for fear of receiving some barb from her sharp tongue. At all events it slipped, falling heavily on to the saucer and sending up into her face and hair great splashes of burning alcohol. I had not been away longer than it took me to replace the bottle into the cupboard, fearing just such an accident, when I heard the noise and the scream and, flying back, found her head on fire like a living sacrifice. Fifille used to sleep on a chair which I always piled up with old pullovers and sweaters so that she should have a soft bed. These I now seized with both hands trying to smother the flames. I wound the knitted garments round her. She moaned softly and I began to fear that I might stifle her. Now her voice came to me as if from a great distance. She said: 'Take care that the house doesn't catch fire!' But fortunately I had removed the bottle. The flames were already extinguished. There was no more alcohol to burn. But when with infinite care I started to unwind the jumpers from her face, strips of skin came away and handfuls of hair, her golden hair. She couldn't open one eye.

We were both prostrated by the suddenness of the accident, and neither of us could remember what to do in the case of such serious facial burns. All that we had been told, or read, evaporated in waves of panic. The emotion had drained the strength from my legs so that I could hardly walk when I went to search for the telephone directory. I then looked for those numbers which I should have known by heart but my vision was too blurred to read them.

The doctor was out visiting, but his assistant told me that I was to put her to bed, give her something to calm her and then paint the burns with mercurochrome. These things I did.

Oh, misery! To think that at last we were beginning to be happy! That I had found a way to amuse her! And that now because of a moment's inattention I had disfigured her. She might even lose an eye. My unhappiness choked me. She was sobbing like a little girl. I wanted to drive quickly down to the chemist, but in my present state I was afraid of having an accident. Then she would be all alone.

The house was as quiet as a few moments ago it had been full of cries and alarms. Why had I allowed her to do this thing? Surely I should have known that there was no strength left in her mutilated hands! But I must go down to the village. I must accept the risks.

When I came back Matilda said to me: 'How quick you have been!'

'I thought you might be anxious.'

'Don't worry. It's no worse than if I had got burnt sun-bathing. But I feel a bit sick.'

I bathed her face with what the chemist had given me, and she fell asleep. Then I went into the kitchen and sat on a chair, alone and miserable. All my happiness was drowned in tears and I felt like writing, as Goya did at the end of his life, *Nada*. Night had fallen. The chickens had gone to roost of their own accord. I remained alone in the kitchen, afraid without anybody to comfort me and to tell me that the

accident was not quite my fault. From time to time I would
peep in at Matilda, and she would say: 'Why, yes, it hurts
but I can bear it. I assure you, it's not too bad.' I knew that
she was lying. The pain must have been atrocious, but she
had learned to suffer stoically. She was accustomed to
suffering. Were her twisted limbs not proof of the suffering
she endured? Why did this atrocious accident have to fall
on her whose cup was already so full? I went up to my room
and put on the radio. There was a play but I couldn't follow
it. Towards midnight I went down to see her again. The
room was in darkness and I groped my way silently.
Suddenly she turned in her bed and shouted violently: 'Get
out!' I broke into tears. So she did think it was my fault!
My very presence had become unbearable. I was being
banished from her room. The tears came up so fast that I
was choking. She made another slight movement and said:
'Oh, it's you, is it? I thought it was the cat who had found
the door ajar and had jumped up on my bed. She gets so
heavy.'

'Does it hurt terribly?' I whispered.

'No, really, no. I think I was asleep. Go back to bed. I'll
be all right tomorrow.'

Sunday dragged. I tuned in to the French Protestant
service at 8.30 a.m. The clergyman exhorted us to patience
and to charity. Matilda was terrible to see. She was scarcely
recognizable, and I felt utterly unstrung.

Mme Javault arrived, as she did every Sunday after Mass,
to collect her eggs.

'Really,' she said, 'your poor mother has no luck. She
was so happy to go about in your little car. She's very
courageous. Just like my husband.' She stood modestly at
the end of the kitchen table and went on: 'It's nearly two
months since he died. He knew that he had only a short

time to live, and now I'm conscience-stricken. I allowed him to do things which were far beyond his strength, and he never complained. He hated the idea of being useless. Your dear mother is just the same.

'Because my husband knew that he had such a short time to live he took his precautions. He filled in my income tax forms for next year and he told me when to renew the radio licence. He wrote me other business letters also. He said: "You only need fill in the date." He said that when he was gone I must untie the dog from the kennel outside and keep him in the house to protect me and to give me better nights. My husband was indispensable to me. As I came home from the village pushing my wheelbarrow up the hill, I would think about all the bits of gossip I had picked up, and I would say to myself: "This or that will amuse him!"

'He used to do so much for me that when he died I was quite helpless. The other day, for instance, I would have liked to put the radio on but I didn't know how to. I had no call to do so, you understand. When we wanted to listen to a little music it was my husband who turned it on. My grandson has since told me what to do. He said: "You must take hold of this knob, Granny, and turn it no more than a hair's breadth!" I laughed when he said that. Fancy! A hair's breadth! But I turned the knob and the music came on. And I felt so proud! Now I listen to the programmes that he and I used to listen to together. Only now it's the dog and I. The dog seems to understand. He barks at everybody else. He's even rather fierce. But with me he's gentleness itself. I rather fancy that my husband must have explained the situation to him beforehand. Dogs can be so intelligent.

'But people like my husband who had no hope of getting better are always having accidents. Last summer, for instance, my husband and I went for a little walk along the sands. He really did it to please me. He didn't want people to say that he was letting himself go, that he didn't make an effort to amuse me. But in order to meet as few people as possible—he would go out like Jean-Jacques Rousseau in an old dressing-gown, and indeed they both had the same illness—we went to that part of the *plage* beyond the bathing tents. Well, suddenly we came upon some moving sands that we didn't even know existed. My husband was soon up to his knees. I had to call out for help. Fortunately some young people who were prawning came and pulled him out. One can do nothing against the unforeseen. Don't think you were responsible for Mme Thibert's accident, Mme Henrey. Life is such a complicated business.'

This then was the manuscript that I found. I had sent it to my husband, and on the back of it I had scribbled these words:

'My darling, I have just spent the most horrible week-end in my life. You can have no idea what this drama has been like. I feel that luck has turned against me now and that all my days will be dark. Away from my son and away from you. I am at this moment utterly undone, but perhaps by the time you receive these words things will be a little better. It's terrible to see Granny. I kiss you. I am dreadfully unhappy. I am beaten. I was far too proud of myself.'

4

I WAS back in London on the first of April. I could not pretend that my mother was any better, and what increased my guilt complex was the unusually cold weather which in the mornings made the unstiffening of her twisted and brittle limbs an even longer and more painful affair. I would have liked to cut down the number of her chickens. She continued to have far too many, but they meant something important to her and made her feel that she still had a useful occupation, and her great joy was to see Mme Javault coming along the garden path to buy her eggs. Now that she could not sew, and her eyes were not strong enough to allow her to read, the chickens alone gave her the illusion of having, like everybody else, a job to do. The danger was that on frosty mornings she could so easily slip in the courtyard leading to the stables.

The first few days in London gave me a feeling of immense peacefulness. The apartment was beautifully warm, and Didi, my Pekinese, gave me such an affectionate welcome. It was nice to feel that he had missed me. Juliette Gréco was in London for a short season at the Savoy Theatre, and Dr Paul Czinner was ready to show his magnificent filming of the *Rosenkavalier*. One needs to come back from time to time to sharpen one's intellect in the heart of a great city. These first April days were also employed in putting down on paper my thoughts about this poignant problem of mother-daughter relationship. The whole thing was so tenuous that if I did not try to analyse it as it was taking place I might not be able to recapture my true feelings. It was an essentially feminine problem which so many other women must come up against.

These April days therefore were used to the full as if I were afraid of misusing them. Was it because they were stolen and I wanted to wring all I could out of them, knowing that they would quickly come to an end? Now that I look back, now that I must try to re-create the atmosphere while I am, alas, all too conversant with the end of the story, what exactly emerges? A recurrence of nightmares, an orgy of new films—some puerile but others excellent—the rather exciting experience of seeing several good plays, the joy of being mistress in my own house. But the cold weather was tiring, and I recall particularly a certain Sunday.

Snow had fallen for several days and my husband was in bed with a chill. I myself had caught an eye infection, for which earlier in the week I had been given some ointment at the High Holborn branch of Moorfields. This admirable eye hospital is one of the few to which one can go without the formality of a doctor's letter. If you are early enough you join the group of people waiting in the casualty department, and it is then just a question of being prepared to wait your turn. An hour or two spent on the long bench in a narrow passage is a sobering experience, and the occasional hurriedly brought-in accident, especially when it concerns a child, is a poignant reminder that one is never sufficiently careful of those in one's care. The nurses of so many races, many of them young with pretty hair and slim waists, are models of kindness, and I was tempted to compare their gentleness and understanding with the brusqueness and ill manners of so many shop assistants in the big stores. The young doctor who examined me diagnosed a number of tiny ulcers, and for a shilling at the dispensary I was given this little box of ointment, which doubtless contained the newest and most costly drugs.

Back at home I felt none of my usual enthusiasm for tidying cupboards, knitting or making something. My eye was painful and the apartment seemed to have collected half the grime of central London. The week-end dragged. At six o'clock on Sunday evening I told my husband that I was going to Mass at Farm Street. My eye was bandaged and, because of the snow, I put a shawl over my head, so that I looked like those women in Cork who on a winter's evening can be seen thus hooded hurrying through the dismal streets.

The great double doors were open so that from the outside one could see the candles brightly flickering on the altar, and this imparted a feeling of warmth to the street scene with its grey houses and half-melted snow. The church was already crowded, but I made my way to the front where it was still possible to squeeze in at the end of a pew. The altar and statues of the Virgin were draped in purple, and suddenly the organ filled the church with majestic notes, and up the aisle came the Cardinal Archbishop of Westminster in his magnificent robes, the congregation kneeling as he passed.

The cardinal seated himself on his throne, a figure of medieval splendour. Time had ceased to have meaning. I had felt old when leaving the flat. Now my thoughts, straying from the words chanted or intoned, disassociated themselves from my body and amused themselves by trying to construct scenes evoked by history books and old paintings whereby the past became the present, for the imagination has no difficulty in eliminating time and space. In such mental exercises, moreover, one is invariably innocent and seventeen. But my bad eye was so painful that I began to wonder if I could stay to the end.

The preacher had gone up into the pulpit and we were listening to his learned sermon. My one good eye was now riveted on the cardinal, and I had the strange impression that he was returning my gaze. His lips also appeared to be moving. Though what I am going to say may sound extraordinary, the pain in my bad eye became less acute and I fell into a torpor. The sermon was a long one, but because I no longer felt much pain all my nervousness had left me.

On my return to the apartment my husband complained that I had been a long time. He had pictured me slipping on the icy roads. He asked me if my eye still hurt.

'When I went to church', I answered, 'I was beginning to wonder if I had a cancer in the eye. You know how apt one is to imagine the worst. I was looking at the cardinal when the pain disappeared. Do you think that miracles can still take place?'

As the days went by I had less and less peace of mind. I continued to sleep badly, but in the morning I drove myself forward determined to live every hour to the full. When, looking back, I consider the use I made of my time I am appalled. On the other hand, who is to be the judge of what is futile and what is not?

I would go to the big stores and perch myself with a feeling of delight on one of those tall stools lined up for the convenience of customers who want to consult voluminous pattern books. This occupation was my joy. I would buy a remnant for a few shillings, and then plan how to turn it into a sleeveless blouse buttoned up the back. Mlle Chanel had indeed facilitated the work of unimaginative sempstresses such as myself. One would think that with the shops so full of cheap blouses, dresses and slips in the brightest colours and superbly cut, set out in a way that one simply can't resist them, we would not want to bother about making our own things. Yet patterns have never sold so well. The answer must be that one method does not harm the other. We buy and we sew. There is room both for

Marks & Spencer and Simplicity Patterns. That is the fun
of living in the present age. Even in countries such as
England, said to be a man's world, every year young woman
is offered more wonders that only a short time ago would
have been as far out of her reach as the jewels of the
Arabian Nights.

My son spent Easter with his granny at Villers. She
must have been immensely touched by this visit, and made
such an effort to reward him for what after all was a natural
desire on his part to be with her that she gave the impression
of being better, I think, than she actually was. Her appetite
had returned and she took pleasure in cooking some of his
dishes on a new electric cooker which I had put in for her
during my last stay. She had a theory that as long as she
remained *un cordon bleu*, and could herself appreciate the
pleasures of the table, there could be nothing very badly
wrong with her.

My grandmother at Blois, in addition to her witchcraft,
had nursed a passion for litigation. Her deafness gave her
the impression that people spoke ill of her. She interpreted
their harmless gossip as malevolent scheming against herself, and even when some neighbour would innocently wish
her good morning she was convinced that it hid an insult.
So she would take them to law, and all the money she earned
would be swallowed up in barrister's fees, so that there was
nothing left to buy food for her girls. Matilda, as a result
of this, had developed a sort of obsessive longing for a loaf of
crisp, golden bread. Having been robbed of the pleasure of
eating her fill of bread in her childhood, she thought in later
life that she could never have enough. When I was a girl she
would confess to me that she could not enter a baker's shop
without being overcome by a furious desire to buy every
loaf in the place—one for every day in her own childhood
when she had gone without. At the farm she would stress on
us the importance of buying a long French loaf every time

we went to the village. Fortunately because of her large farmyard they were never wasted.

The first week in May proved delightful. I was learning to live with what I now acknowledged to be an insoluble problem, and there were evenings when my husband and I would cross London on foot enjoying the spring air, looking at the shop windows, discussing the day's events, on the way to a film or a play. The West End often seemed almost empty after six o'clock. Shop assistants and office workers had gone off by tube and bus to their suburban homes, where by now they were presumably watching television or watering their gardens. The heart of London belonged to a few foreigners and ourselves. I was anxious to see a French film, *Jules et Jim*, partly because of the stir it had made in the artistic world, both in Paris and London, and partly because the role of the Austrian boy was played by a young actor we had known in the Tyrol when my son was making his second film there.

On this particular evening we had an early meal at home and set off in good time for the cinema near Langham Place where the picture was being shown. Flags flew outside the clubs in Charles Street, Mayfair—the Guards Club and the English Speaking Union; the trees in Berkeley Square, fighting bravely against asphyxia from the cars that fought for a parking place against the railings during business hours, were in full leaf and the grass on the lawns was new and green. In Bond Street slept Sotheby's, whose sensational evening auctions, a growing phase of London life, were taking on the appearance of cabaret in a night club. What was left of high society attended these events in evening dress—men and women now half forgotten but who were so very talked about in the period between the wars. One saw them rubbing shoulders, almost timidly, with the *nouveaux riches* of the noisy take-over age, whose halcyon days were even now showing signs of slipping into history. We had been to the sale of the Somerset Maugham pictures, looked dutifully at several millionaires, and left when told that we must watch the auction not in the room where it was taking place but relayed by television elsewhere.

Now we passed Fenwick's, which epitomized all the desires of the modern girl. The window was full of blouses in gay colours with ruffles round the neck and on the sleeves, a delightful fashion that like a ghost was visiting us from the past. Young women wore pants but went feminine in their blouses and their hair-dos. Fashion never ceases to delight and to surprise, and in this respect is far more intelligent than literature, which on occasion, in order to hit the headlines, feels that it must shock, revolt and destroy.

Oxford Street, with the windows of its great stores brilliantly lit, displayed all the wonders of a superlatively wealthy age for the benefit of only a dozen passers-by, a half-empty bus and a bored policeman on his beat. It was as if some great city of the past had emerged from the depths of the ocean to find that there were no humans to people it. If I could have waved a magic wand I would have brought up from the past, from the times of the Tudors and the Stuarts, from the times of Queen Anne and the early Georges, a whole collection of saunterers and street gapers and given them the right to leave their places of abode and come by night to people these brilliant streets emptied by the desires of a modern population to hurry home to television.

Jules et Jim was charming. Jeanne Moreau was the actress of the moment, her immense personality being the artificer of her beauty. She was beautiful even when plain. But it was Oscar Werner who revived memories for me. We had gone to a village in the Tyrol called Thiersee where Karl Hartl, the great Viennese film producer, was to make a picture with my son, who was then nine years old. Because he had a star role we had the privilege of a car, a rather dilapidated Rolls, which was large enough to give lifts to our friends who were less fortunate than we were. Thus when we were not required on the set, or on Sundays, we would pick up Oscar Werner, a member of the Burg Theatre, still in his twenties, and drive to Kufstein or into the fairy-tale villages of Bavaria.

The story of *Jules et Jim* begins when I was a very little girl before and during the First World War, and Jeanne Moreau arrives at a rendezvous wearing a long skirt, a flowered hat and a veil. Through her I saw with a sudden shock Matilda, my mother, wearing just such an outfit and with a long, heavy skirt buttoned down the side. I saw myself also on raw mornings wearing a woollen muffler that became cold and damp because it was too near my mouth. Matilda would insist on propping it up when it slithered down, because she alleged that my throat was weak and that when I began a cold I never could get rid of it. We would be on our way from Clichy to Paris, passing through the great barrier gates in the fortifications, which in those days were intact as during the war of 1870. This was the world of the Douanier Rousseau, toll-gate men with heavy moustaches that smelt of hot red wine and garlic. When we were clear of them we took the Métro to where a certain Mme Réni lived in a sixth-floor room where she made just those long, heavy skirts of which I have spoken. Oh, the pleats and the buttons to sew on—and all for a starvation wage! At midday I was sent out to buy a litre of red wine and fried potatoes for lunch, during the whole of which my mother and Mme Réni did not stop talking about love, money and hats! And when they sewed they sang.

As I watched *Jules et Jim* the scenes in the sixth-floor room, the half-remembered conversations between my mother and Mme Réni, the colour of their clothes, the sound of their voices, even the smell of the wine and the fried potatoes, all became mixed up with the happenings on the screen, and I found myself crying gently for no reason at all. But what I know for certain is that the story of the film became less and less important to me as the scenes of my girlhood and the pictures of Matilda, as she then was, became more vivid and more real. Jeanne Moreau was portraying a much-loved, capricious young woman, and gradually in my mind this character became identified with somebody whom Mme Réni and my mother used often to discuss in the days of my youth. Mme Réni, who was Italian, had left her husband for a lover, who quickly abandoned her, but this did not make Mme Réni think any the less tenderly about love. Women in those days, whether rich or poor, were full of whims and impulses and they existed on love. Every walk in the street was capable of starting an amorous adventure. Everybody walked in those days. Taxis were rare, and the fiacre, with its tired horse, was more often than not an excuse for hidden kisses and tender declarations.

From time to time I would wake up from this reverie and look cautiously at my husband, but he was intent on the film. Then I would try to concentrate once again on what was going on. There is a scene when Jeanne Moreau is married to Oscar and we see them in the chalet with the mountain behind. Jeanne is still wayward and temperamental, so typically a woman of that time. When she goes out on the balcony and sings so tunefully to her husband and to her lover, both of them so desperately in love with her, it is delightful. Afterwards she goes indoors to give instructions to her maid—and the maid's name is Matilda!

'Mathilde! Mathilde!' she cried, and I was startled to hear this name on Jeanne Moreau's lips, the sound filling the theatre, making public what as yet I had kept a secret in my mind. I am not even sure that today I can disentangle the plot of this picture from all that I superimposed upon it. I know that the end was both tragic and farcical. Oscar had grown a little older, but he still had his wild, blond hair. I had seen him again in the car just before Christmas singing *Tannenbaum*, happy because we were all on the point of leaving for Vienna. The first snows had fallen, turning this majestic countryside, with its pine trees and mountains, its valleys and Teuton castles, into a Christmas card scene.

Once again we were in Oxford Street with no desire to take a cab or a bus. Our evening had been a tremendous success, and I had thought so much about my mother that I was beginning to believe that she had come to the picture with us. We talked, we laughed, we reminded each other of the various scenes in the film and of the clothes that Jeanne Moreau wore. When we let ourselves into the flat Didi was there waiting to welcome us. I took him up in my arms and he covered my face with kisses.

But I had another disturbed night. Every time I fell asleep I saw Matilda in my dreams.

As soon as my husband got up in the morning, which was soon after seven, he would take Didi for a walk in the Green Park. Twenty minutes later he would be back with Didi under his arm and a copy of the *New York Times*, which came over from Paris by air every morning. Tuesday started like any other day. My only engagement was to take a friend to a film screening at the Leicester Square Theatre at ten o'clock.

Shortly before this my telephone rang. It was Patsy telling me not to be afraid, but my mother had fallen on the tiles of the kitchen floor on Sunday morning and had been unable to get up by herself. She lay there for several hours until Georgette had looked in at the farm and found her more or less unconscious. Patsy suggested that I should come over as quickly as possible.

My legs folded up under me and it was as if my brain refused to function. I put a call through to my husband, who immediately made himself responsible for my journey. The air service to Deauville had not yet started, and holiday traffic was already beginning to block the normal flights to Paris, and yet I would have to be at the Gare St Lazare in time to catch the 6 p.m. express for Cherbourg. At Lisieux there was a connection for Trouville.

Thus, I thought, while I was amusing myself in London my mother was lying hurt on a cold floor, without help, without any member of her family. I who am so prone to tears couldn't even produce any. My limbs were shaking, and I kept on repeating to myself that if I had taken the night boat from Southampton to Le Havre the previous evening I would already be at her side. My selfishness rose up and choked me.

My husband telephoned the director of Air France, who requisitioned me a seat on the one o'clock flight to Paris. He called for me at home, took me to the bank and drove me to Kensington air station. He had put a call through to Patsy from the office. She had given him the impression that my mother was in a coma.

My journey to Paris was swift and comfortable, and when we landed at Orly the sun came out. I took a taxi to the Gare St Lazare and, as I had two hours to wait, crossed over to the café terrace of the Hotel Terminus, where I ordered a coffee and some croissants.

At this same café terrace I had waited a few days after the liberation of Paris for a train to take me to my farm which I had not seen since the Germans had overrun France five years earlier. Matilda was waiting for me there. She had been in my thoughts during all those cruel years of separation, she on one side of the Channel, I on the other. My husband and I, with my baby, had left her on the quay at St Malo a few hours before the Germans entered the city. Alone and with hardly any money she had made her way to Paris, where she lived miserably, afraid to let it be known that her son-in-law was English, her daughter English by marriage. But it was to my shame, a shame that branded me like a red-hot iron, that we had left her defenceless and alone on French soil, she who had such a profound love for England, who believed that when she was in London nothing really disastrous could happen to her. She liked to think that England was her lucky country. She had never known the poverty here that she had known in Paris. But the immigration authorities at St Malo had not allowed her to get on the ship, because she had a French passport and her visa was not valid. Should I have stayed with her on that occasion? That was the beginning of my guilt complex. That was the facet of this eternal problem which had harassed me relentlessly during all the bombing and the second front. Was I an unnatural daughter?

But when after the liberation of Paris I had sat at this café terrace waiting for a train to take me to her I had at least been happy. Hope was what buoyed me up. I was going to see her again after this long, cruel separation. There would be years of happiness, I said to myself, stretching ahead. Now that the war was over nothing else mattered. We would not allow ourselves to be separated again. Yes, that is what I said and yet look what had happened! I had been twice an undutiful daughter. This spring, knowing that she needed me, I had put the Channel between us. She had had a nasty fall while I was there. She was bound to slip again on the kitchen tiles. Was I so hard-hearted that being aware of this I had coldly left her to her fate?

The man sitting opposite me in the Cherbourg express

was going to Caen, where he had been responsible for rebuilding much of the stricken city. The work was nearly finished, he said, and the new city was very fine. The old one, with its narrow streets and picturesque centuries-old houses, was unhealthy. The sanitation dated from medieval times. Yes, the new one was very fine, but like all new cities a trifle dull. But it was no good regretting the past. Modern cities might be less fun, but it was better to be alive than under the ruins of the old ones. The problem was to know what to do with oneself in the evening.

'Where are you going?' he asked suddenly.

'Deauville,' I answered.

'Change your mind and spend the evening with me at Caen. There are some remarkable restaurants. We'll have a memorable dinner and afterwards I'll show you some of the things I've been doing. Unless I'm mistaken you have an inquisitive turn of mind. It will amuse you and I won't have to spend a dull evening all by myself.'

I told him that my business at Deauville could not be put off. At Lisieux he very courteously helped me with my bags, and forty minutes later the local train brought me to my destination.

Patsy was waiting for me at the barrier.

'Oh,' she cried, 'I love your white coat!'

This piece of futility cut me even harder than the cold wind coming in from the sea. Was it her way of hiding the news I most feared?

'Mother?' I gasped. 'How is she?'

'No change,' she said.

'Conscious?'

'Yes, quite conscious.'

We drove along the coast road. I must have had a fever, for my lips were so parched that I had the impression that the skin was cracking. The road was deserted. At times the wind howled across it, throwing up little mountains of dry sand.

'Your car is at Montauzan,' said Patsy. 'All you need do is to jump into it and go home.'

The gate was open and I drove straight into the orchard. My house was brilliantly lit—this house that when I first set eyes on it obscurely housed farmer Goguet and his family. I have a curious mind that plays tricks on me. As I bounced and jolted down the grass road with the twisted apple trees on both sides of me, these lines of Victor Hugo suddenly came rushing upon me:

> Il est nuit. La cabane est pauvre mais bien close,
> Le logis est plein d'ombre, et l'on sent quelquechose
> Qui rayonne à travers ce crépuscule obscur—
> Des filets de pêcheur son accrochés au mur.

Hugo, of course, was talking about a fisherman's cabin in Brittany. But I know now why at this poignant moment my brain brought back these lines from the past. As a girl I was made to learn them by heart and, because children invariably put their own interpretations on the work of grown-ups, I had substituted Milou, my father, for Victor Hugo's fisherman, and when

> La porte tout à coup s'ouvrit, bruyante et claire,
> Elle fit dans la cabane entrer un rayon blanc;
> Et le pêcheur, trainant son filet ruisselant,
> Joyeux, parut au seuil . . .

I saw my father standing joyously on the threshold, not with a fisherman's net as in the poem but with a sackful of broken wood, as I remember him so often, when he came back from a day's work on a building site. I could just see my mother looking up critically from her sewing, her narrow lips pursed as Milou put the sack down roughly on her newly waxed floor.

I switched off the engine of my car and hurried into the house.

A woman whom I recognized as belonging to the village sat at the end of the kitchen table at the very place where I always saw Matilda sitting either when I arrived or when I left to go back to London. This was the first time that I had ever been obliged to face the fact that in my absence Matilda might not be mistress in my house. My mother's door was ajar and I heard her say: 'I'm thirsty.'

I went quickly into her room. She was in bed propped up against a pile of pillows. I knelt down and kissed her and she recognized me right away. I took off my coat and said to the woman in the kitchen: 'I'm home now and I shall look after her. Please leave the house.'

I gave her more money than she asked for in order to get rid of her as quickly as possible. Even so she took far too long to go. I was impatient to be alone with Matilda. Mother and daughter. Mother and daughter.

I put some water to her lips. She went to sleep a few moments later, and when she woke again it was only to murmur, 'I've such a bad head!' and to ask for another drink of water.

I pulled up a chair beside her bed and took up some knitting which I had left unfinished at the end of my last stay. Occasionally she would open her eyes and look at me, and although my throat was parched I forced myself to appear unconcerned and to talk to her in the most natural way. Her voice, when she answered me, was the same as usual. It had become the clear, youthful voice that I remembered as a little girl and which until this moment I had quite forgotten.

The night proved long and hard. She pleaded with me not to put her on a bed pan but to let her get up. Her back was covered in sores, and because the doctor had cut out the more powerful modern drugs her limbs had stiffened. However, her desire to help was touching.

'Since the doctor forbade me cortisone,' she said, 'I find

it twice as hard to move, but I'll sit on the edge of the bed and count three. Then I'll make a big effort to get up. That's what I've been doing lately. For the last month I have hardly dared to lie down at night for fear of not being able to get up in the morning.'

At about 3 a.m. I was driven by exhaustion and bitter cold to seek a short rest on my own bed, but I was too over-wrought to sleep, and every time I came down to see Matilda I found her collapsed across her bed, having tried during my short absence to go to the toilet rather than to use what she termed the odious bed pan. I would than have to change her sheets and try to make her comfortable again, but there were moments when I became so discouraged that I broke into tears. The weight of her emaciated body was more than I could manage and my efforts to lift her seemed almost cruel.

Soon after eight Georgette arrived, and a little later a nurse who worked part time at a hospital at Deauville but who was not free when Patsy had sent for her the previous day. Between us we soon made my mother comfortable.

When the nurse had gone Georgette said: 'It must have been about four o'clock on Sunday morning when your mother fell. Unfortunately there was a lot of work to do at the farm and it was late when I arrived. Though the sun was up the lights were on and the door was locked. I could see your mother lying on the floor. She told me to break a pane and turn the key in the door, but as her bedroom window was 'open I crawled in that way.

'Your mother was lying full length on the floor. Her clothes were wet and soiled and she was frozen. I managed to sit her up on a chair and then ran back to Berlequet to fetch Jacques, and together we put her back into bed. "All I want is to feel warm again," she said. We gave her some hot-water bottles and she drank a little warm milk. Then I went to fetch Mme Poirot at Montauzan.

'Madame and I gave her a change of clothes. "What a lot of trouble I'm giving you," she said plaintively to Mme Poirot. "I'm sure Mme Owen doesn't give you half so much work!" But as soon as we left her alone for a moment she would try to get up, and then she would fall down and we had to start all over again. That's why we had to get a nurse, but the one who is here now couldn't come and we had to settle for the woman you found last night. I would have stayed with her myself if it hadn't been that we had two cows about to calve, and Mme Poirot couldn't leave her mother for more than a little while. And she also has the baby. So you see that we could only do a little, but now that you have arrived everything will be all right."

I spent most of the second night changing my mother's sheets and washing mountains of soiled linen which I discovered stacked all over the place. For how long would I have the strength to go on like this? I sent up little prayers to heaven asking for the strict minimum so that I should not have to send her away.

When I had time to sit beside her she went on talking to me in that half-forgotten voice. Listening to her I began to remember whole snatches of conversation, she sewing, I on the floor. She used to tell me, for instance, about her own childhood, how she never had any of the things that other children had, and how she would stand in front of a toy shop in the Rue Denis Papin at Blois and long so desperately for something from the gay window display: a doll or a cot or a doll's tea-set. And when I was very little I would say to her: 'If I had known you then, I would have given you half my toys. And we would have gone to school together and I would have protected you from all the horrible children who laughed at your red hair and called you "Ginger!"' My enthusiasm made her laugh and she would answer me in that same childish, high-pitched voice that had suddenly come back to her now.

I now reminded her of these things, and from time to time, using the patois of her youth, she would say 'Ben oui' or 'Ben non', and the look in her eyes would be both artless and malicious.

I bent over her and I tried to speak to her as I spoke to her when I was a child. She lifted a hand and tried to push aside a lock of my hair which had fallen across my eyes as she did when I was little, and occasionally she grasped me by the wrist as she so often did when I came home from school, eager to make sure that I hadn't got a temperature, for she was always haunted by the fear that she could lose me as she had lost my baby brother.

Patsy came to see me the next evening at about seven. When she went into my mother's room my mother called out: 'Ah, so it's you, Patsy!' And when Patsy had gone my mother started to tell me what had happened in the village during my absence.

'Did you know', she asked, 'that Mme Javault's grand-daughter, Michèle, is three months' gone? That will give her two babies to look after. It's because her husband came home on leave from the army. It's always like that when the men come home on leave.'

I told her that just before leaving London, Julius Meller, the silk merchant for whom so many years ago I worked as a junior secretary in Aldermanbury in the City, had written to me out of the blue. He had just read a book in which I had mentioned his name. He invited me to lunch near his new office in Soho. It was rather fun to remember how frightened I had been of him, and how annoyed he used to make me when at five minutes to six, knowing that I had a date waiting for me outside, he would begin dictating long letters to his silk merchants in Lyons. We tried to pretend that neither of us had changed, and in a way, except that I was no longer afraid of him, that was true, for it was the easiest thing in the world to take up our parts again like actors and see each other as we were. At that time, of course, I had been living with my mother in Stacey Street, and as I used to tell her every single thing that happened to me at work she now had no difficulty in recalling the name of Julius Meller.

She listened for a few moments with interest and then said: 'So you were pleased to see him?'

'Yes,' I answered, 'and what's more he gave me a very pretty silk square. He says that silk squares have become quite an important thing in his import business.'

'Naturally,' said my mother with the air of a person who doesn't need the obvious pointed out; 'they have replaced the hats and fur collars of my youth.'

All this was very encouraging. But she was seldom the same for two minutes on end. For suddenly she would say like a petulant child: 'I want my soup!'

I would hurry away and make some, but when I brought it to her the desire had flown and she would scarcely take a spoonful. She was already thinking about something else. I had put Fifille at the foot of her bed, and the little dog, seeing the bowl of soup, began to wag her tail.

'Oh,' cried my mother, 'how funny she looks!' And she broke into delicious ripples of laughter like a little girl.

Night, as far as I was concerned, was merely a prolongation of the day, and in order to prevent myself from sleeping I would put great pails of dirty linen to boil on the Aga stove. I would go from room to room trying to bring a semblance of normality back into my house, but always my tired steps would lead me back to Matilda's bedside. I took to changing her as I would have changed a baby, but the sound of her cries each time I touched her brought fresh tears to my burning eyes.

I made fresh coffee in the morning and took her a great bowl of it, half milk, half coffee, piping hot with lots of sugar.

'My goodness,' she exclaimed, 'how good it is! I haven't tasted coffee like this for a long time.'

I kissed her lightly on the forehead. Normally she disliked any demonstration of affection, but I said 'Kiss me!' and she kissed me without demurring. I even went so far as to ask, with a slight tremor in my voice: 'Do you love me?'

'Of course I love you,' she said. 'I'm giving you enough trouble, aren't I?'

I don't know what possessed me at that moment, but I wanted to push my advantage home like somebody straining on a cord until it snaps. I said: 'You remember your baby son?'

'Of course!'

'And Marie-Thérèse? Do you remember her?'

'Yes.'

'And do you know who I am?'

She laughed and said: 'Ben, La Madeleine!'

'Yes,' I said, 'I'm your daughter.'

'My daughter?' she said. 'Have I got a daughter?'

And then, of course, my heart broke and I began to weep. Why could I not leave well alone? Why did I have to go on questioning her until I had made her express surprise that she could have a daughter? In order to lead her gently back into the paths of reason, I said, almost light-heartedly: 'As soon as you're better we'll go for another drive in the car.'

She gave me a knowing look and answered: 'Yes, yes, but you would need to have a car, and you haven't got one.'

Her mind was back in the days, not so long ago, when I laboriously bicycled between the farm and the village, bringing up all the provisions in a basket between the handle-bars. I had kept her waiting too long for her drives. In this also I was to blame. She had forgotten the good days. They had come too late.

And yet I had once taken her in my little Citroën to Ver-sur-Mer, where in 1918 I was sent with some of the other girls of my Protestant school at Clichy to a holiday camp. It was at Ver-sur-Mer that I saw the sea for the first time. We lodged in a large house with a big garden overlooking the wide stretch of golden sand. Our dormitories were cool and agreeable; the refectory was composed of a long table with straw-backed chairs; at the head of the table we found a pile of New Testaments, hymn books, and a long, sharp bread knife. For breakfast we had bowls of milk and coffee, and after prayers we were free to go to the sands. We would come back when the churches of Ver, of Asnelles and of Arromanches sounded the angelus. Their deep tones were impressive in the calm of the fields. The sea grumbled distantly.

Could my mother have forgotten this pilgrimage to the tiny *plage* which had made such a deep impression on her daughter's youthful years? For me that holiday camp had been the calm after four years of war-weary Paris. Oh, how I talked to my mother about it when I was back in our hot, airless flat in Clichy! But, of course, when we arrived, my mother and I, in the little car we discovered that there was nothing left of the large house with the big garden—or indeed of the village! The allied bombardments in the Second World War and the landings had utterly destroyed it. But I was able to show Matilda the spot from which I had first seen the sea, and we even discovered the farm, or what was left of it, where we used to buy our milk. The farm was pretty, and when the woman was not there we used to play with her little boy of three whom we covered with kisses. One evening when we were crossing the cornfield with our milk-pails we heard, instead of the angelus, a lugubrious tolling, and we became sad, so near seemed death in the quiet of the country. When we reached the farm we discovered that the bell was tolling for the little boy, who that afternoon had been drowned in a cattle pool.

Could my mother have forgotten that? She was asleep now but after a while she opened her eyes and said: 'Tout passe, tout casse!' She repeated it twice, and I wondered what memory deep in her half-conscious brain had made her murmur this old saying about everything passing, everything coming to an end.

Sunday was Mothers' Day. Georgette came in the morning and offered to stay with Matilda while I went down to the village. All the shops were open and it was very gay. I took Brigitte with me. She asked me if I would like to know what her great ambition of the moment was? A plastic basket in which to put the mussels she intended to go looking for at the next low tide. Her mother would make them into a delicious soup with milk and cream. I asked her if it had to be plastic. Wouldn't an osier one be prettier? No, she said with a touch of scorn in her young voice, plastic was newer.

Our village was beginning to endear itself to me because so many of the young girls serving in the shops had been born on our farms. My neighbours the Poulins, for instance, had five little girls whom I had known since they learned to take their first steps, clinging tightly to their grandmother, Mme Castel. I had even been called in to help when one of them was born. Annick, who had become very pretty, now worked at the baker's shop and served us our crisp French loaves, and even when the tiny shop was crowded with summer visitors, Annick would give me that special smile, which was her way of telling me that I was not just any customer. Yvette, the eldest, worked at the haberdasher's and served me with elastic and knitting wool. When she was very little she might have died if it hadn't been that my own house had the telephone. A farm servant upset a bowl of soup over her and she was so badly scalded that her father, out of his mind, burst in upon me for help. We telephoned to Dr Lehérissey, who saved her with penicillin. That night none of us slept. She now had a very becoming hair-do which hid the scar.

We saw many children walking rather self-consciously through the streets carrying a plant. Brigitte told me that she was going to buy one for her Granny Rosalie with whom they were going to lunch. To her mother she would give cut flowers. She added very seriously: 'They are very expensive this year because of the frost!' The pastrycook shops were also very busy. Quite obviously nobody was going to forget Mothers' Day. Neither must I forget that little girls as well as mothers find the pastrycook's window an irresistible attraction. We would go in and choose a cake for Brigitte.

Suddenly the word 'pastrycook' caused me to cry: 'Eureka!' Now I suddenly remembered how my stepafther Thibert, the pastrycook from Lyons, used to repeat endlessly as he made his *gaufrettes* at Stacey Street: 'Tout passe, tout casse!' Everything was going to be better after the Derby, but alas nothing ever did get better for him, neither after the Derby nor after Ascot, nor even Goodwood. But it came to me as something of a shock that my mother might have been thinking of her second husband when I had felt so certain that she had been reliving our existence at Clichy with me small and my father Émile in the background. It pained me a little because it seemed to show that there was a barrier between our thoughts. As soon as I got back to the farm I released Georgette from her vigil, and after putting the provisions away went to sit beside my mother. I wanted her to drink something but she refused it, and though she occasionally opened her eyes she would almost immediately fall back into a deep sleep.

In the afternoon as Matilda continued to sleep I closed up the house and drove to Montauzan.

Patsy's mother was in her room sitting in front of a large tapestry frame. She could, of course, only work with her left hand, but she looked like a queen in a fairy story, her white hair braided, her back very straight. Courageously she was trying to exercise her paralysed limbs.

'If only you knew how much I've been thinking about you!' she cried. 'I'm so unhappy not to be able to go and see your mother. You must be patient. Your mother is very ill, but she may live a long time yet. Don't tire yourself out. That's important. I'm very well versed in these matters, for I am of a generation who kept the members of a family at home till the last moment. I had my grandmother, my mother and several aunts. One must learn to face up to one's responsibilities without fear. It's the woman's role in life.'

My visit could only be a short one. I had brought her some English magazines and I knew that she would be glad to look at them. She was in no pain. That was the secret of her gentle philosophy, her quiet optimism.

Matilda on my return was still asleep. Her room was in the oldest part of the house and her large window was cut into a wall at least four feet deep, a wall of smooth stones which stalwart men in the days of our Mary Tudor probably brought up in carts from the beach. That is how they built four hundred years ago.

On this alcove I had placed a great number of geraniums which had spent the winter indoors. On Granny's window they would be half in, half out, slowly getting accustomed to the open air. But the chickens who became impudent when Granny was alone in the house would hop over the garden fence and come to pick at the young geranium leaves on her window sill.

'They know I'm no longer strong enough to chase them away,' said Granny rather sadly. 'They dig up your poor geraniums. I kept a big stick beside my bed, and when the birds jumped on to the window I made a great show of beating the stick on the ground. When I first did that they all flew away cackling. They were terrified. But gradually they realized that I couldn't reach them with my stick and so they no longer took any notice. And now your plants are in a sorry plight.'

It was to preserve her dignity that she had refused until the very last moment to take to her bed.

The kitchen was warm and there was a great pile of linen to rinse and to hang out on the line. I turned on the television and immediately life came surging into my house from the outside world. Television, radio and electric light did much to rob my apprehension and they made my loneliness possible to bear.

I carried the clean linen into the *patio* where the washing line stretched from the stable roof to a young apple tree fifty yards away, but since my last visit I had to get up on a wheelbarrow to reach the line. The fault lay with the apple tree, which had grown by more than a foot, taking the line with it so that now it was just out of my reach. The innocent tree, covered in pink apple blossom and looking like a bride had an air of virginal pride. Every time that I pinned a sheet on to the line both I and the sheet were covered in blossom. My tree was very beautiful and I was the guilty one for having harnessed its bough to a washing line!

Matilda's chickens all came pecking round me. Whenever I came out into the *patio* they followed me wherever I went, happy in my company, interested in my various activities. I had gone to fetch them at the station when they were little balls of fluff, and I had opened the box in which they were packed on the kitchen table while our two cats, Celestina and Mitou, perched on the Aga, had looked with their slit, orange eyes at this appetizing mass of babyhood. Matilda took them all up in turn in her twisted, knotty hands to kiss them and feel their softness against her cheeks. We had put them in the stables where they had grown up against the warmth of the electric heaters which replaced their mothers and now they were more than friendly. But, alas, I had been obliged to take a cruel decision. I had no time with my mother so ill to look after them and Jacques had made arrangements to sell all but four. A man was coming to fetch my dear Rhode Island Reds tomorrow. The wooden boxes were already here.

That Sunday evening I tried to relax by working late in the garden, cutting the grass and weeding the paths, but that only lasted till about eight o'clock, and then I went into the kitchen to switch on the television in the hope that whatever was going on would be sufficiently exciting to hold my interest. The door leading to Matilda's bedroom was ajar and I soon found myself trying to listen to her breathing. Guilty about the noise the television was making I cut it off. By ten o'clock I was so tired that I decided that I must do something if I didn't want to fall asleep on a chair. I gave my mother something to drink and asked her if she was in pain.

'Oh yes,' she answered softly.

She had opened her eyes and was looking at me, and I noticed that her eyes, instead of being red and inflamed as they had been for several months, had suddenly become a beautiful clear blue. I began to feel more hopeful and even wondered if this sharp attack might not in the end do good to her eyes.

The sore on her back was raw and must have been

terribly painful. I changed her and put clean sheets on the bed. Propped up against the pillows, with the reading lamp carefully shaded, she looked more comfortable. I sat in the armchair at the head of her bed, but my own back was painful and I was dreadfully cold.

She took up so little space in her bed, and she did not move at all except occasionally an arm, so I slipped into the bed beside her and put my head against her shoulder. She now had an arm round me, and from time to time her hand would bury itself in mine. I could hear her heart beating. I was warm and I was doing something which in normal circumstances I would never have dared to do—cuddle up like a little girl against my mother. Not for years had I felt so enveloped in tenderness and love and in the happiness of being together, daughter and mother, two women united in maternal and filial affection. Now at last I could give myself to her in full measure, without fear or timidity, without awkwardness or any thought of ridicule.

I would have liked this night to last for ever. From time to time I fell asleep but would soon wake up with a start, fearing that I had failed in my duties towards her. Then I would discover her hand in mine and all would be well.

Dawn was breaking and from all the neighbouring farms one could hear the cocks crowing. I raised myself on an elbow and looked at Matilda. She seemed calmer and her breathing was, if anything, more regular than mine. We had both enjoyed a wonderful night.

My instinct, of course, was to get up and let the chickens out, but I suddenly remembered that Jacques had told me that I must not do so. They would quickly, following their breakfast, scatter across the orchards and he would not be able to catch the ones I had so reluctantly decided to sell and which he was to put in the waiting boxes. The break-up of Matilda's farmyard made me feel immensely sad. I think that my affection for her chickens was to a great extent because they made such a lot of life round the house. Even when they wrecked my kitchen garden I forgave them as one forgives a child who breaks something valuable in the house. When they all trooped out into the orchards they were as joyous as a band of schoolgirls skipping and laughing during the morning break.

Fifille was on heat and had run off during the night. I called her but there was no answer. The previous day half a dozen dogs from the surrounding farms had come to the garden gate, yelping and howling for her. I was furious. They had frightened me with their lugubrious barking and had set me thinking of the hound of the Baskervilles.

I now, as I so often did during this period, tried to give my house an appearance of normality. I went to fetch coke for the Aga. I brought the linen in from the *patio* and ironed it. I put a new consignment of dirty washing to soak and to boil. I put on the radio to get the news from England. And then there was a scratching at the kitchen door, and Fifille, her fur all ruffled up, slunk in. She jumped on to her chair, curled herself up on the cushions and was soon fast asleep and snoring.

5

THE transistor on the kitchen table was tuned in to the news. This, said the man in England, was Monday, 28th May. My grandmother at Blois was of the opinion that it was unwise to consult the oracle on the day of the moon. It was a bad day, she said. Was it from her that I had inherited this unwholesome interest in old wives' tales and superstitions?

Jacques and Georgette came down the orchard on their tractor. I went out to meet them and all three of us proceeded immediately to the stables, where we were to put Matilda's chickens in the wooden cages already stacked against the wall. The unfortunate creatures must have been waiting impatiently for the moment when I would release them and throw them their grain, when they could drink from the trough of clear water in the middle of the *patio*, and then hurry off to their favourite haunts for another full and exciting day in the surrounding orchards. But when we opened the stable doors it was to set upon them and try to press them into cages. The presence of Jacques and Georgette in this confined space took them by surprise. They were not used to strangers. And now all this stalking, this brutality, this noise, drove them crazy with fear and must have come to them as a terrifying warning of their doom. Stirred by sudden remorse I allowed more than I should have done to escape. I had restarted a farmyard in 1946 with four chickens as black as jackdaws and a young turkey who was just as black as they were. The chickens had produced a curious race of various shades of grey and beige. Every time new chicks were hatched Matilda and I gave little shouts of surprise. All our farms had the same inbred birds because of the German occupation. Matilda gave our hens individual names as if they had been cows. There was La Grisotte, La Beigeotte, La Blanchotte, names that delighted my child when he was little. Granny, like her mother, invented a language of her own (with many words peculiar to the Berry and the valley of the Loire) in which she spoke both to her grandson and to her chickens. When La Beigeotte had chicks they became Les Beigeoux or Les Bigeonnets, and the descendants of La Blanchotte became Les Blanchounnets. And so on. They were less hens than important persons.

My son, when he grew a little older, bought his Granny beautiful Leghorns whose white plumage delighted her. They were elegant and very interested in everything. Later we had Sussex and finally these Rhode Island Reds because of their brown eggs. The purer the race, however, the less we could tell them apart. They ended by losing their personalities. 'Tout passe. Tout casse.'

Jacques and Georgette swung the cages containing Matilda's hens on to the tractor. They were accustomed to selling living animals off their farm, and for poultry they had no time because it was not even a profitable sideline. My poor Rhode Island Reds, boxed in, pressed tightly together, hardly able to breathe, did not let out the slightest sound. Their excited clucking was over. Between the wooden bars they gazed longingly at the green orchard where they had been brought up, where they had spent such long happy days and which they would never see again, while those whom I had allowed to escape appeared even more frightened, and I almost think that if they had been able to, they would have rushed to join their doomed sisters.

The tractor made off, Jacques and Georgette bareheaded

at the prow, so young, so full of strength, like two young Romans bound for a new conquest.

I went back to the kitchen. I felt cold and terribly alone. I longed to talk to my mother who remained so quietly in her bed, and it seemed such a short time since the days when there was nothing I did that she didn't comment on, nothing that I wanted to do upon which I did not first ask her advice.

I felt suddenly old and fragile.

The nurse arrived and once again we changed Matilda and made her bed, but though we spoke to her she did not seem to hear us. We were facing each other across the light sleeping body and we started to exchange village news.

Suddenly Fifille began to bark angrily. This generally meant that we had a male visitor, for she was not accustomed to their deep voices and would try to stop them from coming into the house. As I entered the kitchen I saw the stocky figure of our postman, who was arriving long before the time when he normally brought the letters.

'I'm bringing Mme Thibert's pension,' he announced.

The pension which the French Government paid Matilda was called *L'Aide aux Economiquement Faibles*. It had been designed to help those who had reached a certain age and were living at home, but who, never having been in regular employment, could not claim the much higher benefits that retired workers enjoyed under the various state insurance schemes. Matilda was very proud of her pension, which she made use of to pay her doctor. Her drugs had by now become so costly that they had to be met from quite a different source, but this did not spoil her almost childish satisfaction in being in part self-supporting.

I told the postman that my mother was very ill. As it was one of his functions to deliver old age pensions to those who were entitled to them he was no doubt accustomed to finding many of them ill in bed. He said: 'It won't make any difference your mother being ill, Mme Henrey. Just get her to sign the receipt.'

'I don't think she's strong enough,' I said.

The postman was gently insistent. 'You've only got to hold her hand and guide her,' he said.

The nurse and I propped Matilda comfortably against her pillows, and I took her hand in mine and helped her to form the letters of her name. Her hand was warm and dry, very pleasant to hold. I said: 'It's for your pension. You're pleased, aren't you?'

I went back to the kitchen to hand the paper to the postman, who had already counted out the money, and when he had gone smiling happily because of the few francs I had given him, pursued by Fifille barking as furiously as ever, I put the notes in the drawer of the kitchen table where Matilda kept her personal treasures. The nurse was preparing to leave. She advised me to put a few drops of glycerine on my mother's lips, and as I was doing so Georgette came back to fill up the Aga and do some cleaning.

I half expected the doctor, but he didn't come.

I drove down to the village to get some petrol just in case something happened and I had to use the car urgently. I was beginning to realize that the moment might come when I would be obliged to take Matilda to a nursing home in Deauville. I did not dare ask myself how long my own strength would last. My inadequacy appalled me. To make matters worse the weather during these last few days of May remained bitterly cold.

On my return home I missed the noise and gaiety of Matilda's Rhode Island Reds, who normally at this hour would have been at the foot of the big pear tree in front of the garden gates. The few whose lives I had saved were huddled pitifully together in a corner of the *patio* still terrified by what they had witnessed early in the morning, and not knowing what to make of so much empty space, so much food in the overflowing grain troughs. They were ill at ease, filled with an unknown fear. Normally our birds, like schoolgirls, divided up into gangs of friends and went off joyfully to explore the countryside. These few unhappy creatures were probably not friends at all, but had merely been thrown together by circumstance.

I had been obliged also to get rid of Matilda's cats. My house therefore was a place of sadness, a place of continual apprehension in which the only creature to be contented was Fifille, who not only jumped on Granny's bed from time to time but also had me, her mistress, to pet her, to talk to her and to take her out in the car whenever I went to the village.

The church clock in the village struck midday. Georgette had gone home. I made a pot of tea and decided to have a boiled egg. I had a good supply of eggs, all those I had collected the previous evening before the birds were taken away. Mme Javault would not be coming for them. I had already warned her that our arrangement must come to an end, and I fancy that she had already made other plans, though it was not easy to buy farm eggs any longer. The farmers' wives, whose perquisite it used to be, no longer found it profitable, and the new generation of customers could not tell the difference between farm eggs and those produced in batteries.

I was so nearly on the point of despair that to give myself courage I began telling my mother what I had done in the village, but she did not even open her eyes. I warmed her a little milk but it hurt her to swallow.

I started to tidy the kitchen and told myself that this was a good opportunity to make the changes which I never dared do when Matilda was watching me. There was, for instance, a whole range of aluminium pans, many battered, which for several months I had been longing to throw away. I had brought beautiful stainless steel ones from England. In London I would not cook in anything else. But Matilda had liked aluminium pans in which to concoct those queer dishes for her cats, claiming that they were lighter for her poor hands to lift. But now the cats had gone and I would have to do our cooking myself. In spite of the continual heat of the Aga I was still shivering. I would get some anthracite and light the furnace. I might feel better if the central heating was on.

All this time I kept up a running conversation with Matilda through the open door of her room. Occasionally I would break off what I was doing and run in to her and kiss her. I treated her as if she were a baby, my baby asleep in bed. I wondered if the doctor might come after all. I ironed several pairs of sheets and put them away in the cupboard in Matilda's room. Occasionally I switched on the radio and then almost immediately turned it off.

There were two window boxes painted sky blue which last summer, filled with geraniums, had looked very pretty in the alcove of my mother's deep stone window. A little gardening might help to get me warm. I changed the earth in the window boxes and then transferred into it some of the geraniums that were still in the pots in which they had spent the winter. As my mother had warned me, they were a good deal damaged by those impudent hens who had, alas, paid so dearly for their minor crimes. My mother's windows were wide open and I could keep watch over her while in the garden planting the geraniums. Her breathing soon became heavy—too much so. At four o'clock I went back into the house and decided to sit beside her bed.

I was uncertain what to do. From time to time I stroked her cheek. Then I would make her sip some water. I felt an

urge to pass my fingers lightly over her dear face. I remembered over the long, long years the noise my father, Milou,
made when he was dying. I also recalled a certain night in a
ward at the Westminster Hospital when a woman in the bed
next to mine was in the death struggle. No, Matilda was not
making that strange noise.

But I no longer dared to leave her.

Fifille was curled up asleep at the foot of her bed. A tit
came to peck at a piece of bread that I had left by her window. The birds came right into the house now that the cats
were gone. I was terribly afraid and yet at the same time
there was a strange peace within me. Something made it
impossible for me to get up from my chair. Once or twice
I propped Matilda up against the pillows to ease her
breathing, but she didn't appear to be in any pain. Her hands
were a little whiter, and those dark veins which ran across
them like snakes had subsided so that her hands looked
younger. I thought it might be due to the rest she had been
having in bed. Her hair was still bronze, the colour of fire.
This very morning the nurse had remarked on its beauty.

I struggled against an overwhelming desire to sleep. In
the end I forced myself to get up and make some very
strong tea. The house was incredibly still. I brought my cup
to Matilda's bedside and tried to make her drink a few
drops, but unsuccessfully. I then took up my knitting, but
my desire to stroke her face came on again. I took her hand
in mine and noticed once again how agreeable it was to the
touch—dry, soft and warm. Her pulse beat evenly.

This was the moment, I think, when I really felt abandoned by all those whom I loved. They were in London
going about their normal occupations, laughing, running
after buses, or perhaps in their offices preparing to go home.
Exactly a week ago I also had been in London, crossing
Piccadilly with Didi in my arms, thinking about the film I
was going to see with my husband. Crowds of office

workers streamed across the Green Park from the Ritz
Hotel to Buckingham Palace. They were hurrying to catch
trains at Victoria station. That is what they would also be
doing at this very moment. My mind pictured the familiar
London landmarks—the Ritz Hotel, Arlington House,
those two new blocks of luxury flats, which made me a little
jealous when I saw their french windows and wide balconies, the new Stornaway House, built on the site of Lord
Beaverbrook's old home, and the corner house with the
green shutters which belongs to Lord Rothermere. People
would be buying evening papers, rushing into tube stations,
queueing at bus stops, looking at share prices, happy at the
thought of being reunited with their families, of supper,
television, a long chat before bed.

At six o'clock I went to fetch the transistor to put on the
news. Matilda showed no sign of waking up and this surprised me. A new wave of fear came over me and I began to
shiver again. Nothing I did could dispel this absence of
bodily warmth. I doubt if I even heard the headlines of the
news, and very soon I switched the radio off.

Matilda was still breathing with difficulty and the sound
of her respiration seemed to fill the house, rather like the
noise of distant waves breaking on a sandy beach.

Suddenly she let out a long-drawn sigh, and a few
seconds later another one longer than the first. Then all
became still. Completely still. I uncovered her chest and put
an ear against her heart. There was no sound at all. Only
absolute silence. I seized her in my arms and cried out:
'Maman! Maman! Maman!' I covered her forehead and her
cheeks with kisses. For the first time I could do all this
without hurting her. She had ceased to know the meaning
of pain. She had said to me more than once: 'Don't feel sad
when I die. I shall be relieved not to suffer any more.' I felt
suddenly full of joy that she had ceased to be racked by
pain. She was finally at peace. I kept on taking her in my

arms and hugging her. My legs had given way under me and my heart was beating so much that I felt that it was capable of breaking my ribs.

I knew that I was no longer the person I had been only a minute earlier. No other woman of her age would ever call me 'thou' again. These one-syllable words 'thou' and 'thee' had suddenly become precious to me—marvellous. Like the word 'mother' itself. I began slowly to assess my loss, my utter confusion. From the church in the village down by the sea came the sounds of the angelus and I knew that it must be seven o'clock. My mother had already begun her first evening in Eternity, and I was beginning one of solitude. She and I had spent fifty-five years together. I would never know such a space of time again.

A car was coming down the orchard.

The engine was switched off, a door slammed and I hurried out to see Patsy arriving with her daughter Anne. I said to her in English: 'Don't bring the child. Mother has just died.'

The words half choked me.

'Ah!' she said.

She sent Anne back to the car and came into the house with me.

'Shall I stay?' she asked.

'No, thank you, Patsy. I want to be with her for as long as I can. But go and tell Longuet, the carpenter, because tomorrow there's a nation-wide strike of electricity and he'll be hampered in his work.'

I had already to think of what comes hand in hand with death.

I listened to her driving back across the orchard. I telephoned the doctor and then put in a call to London. Please heaven there should be an answer. The offices would only just be closing. My husband might not be home yet. But he was.

His voice calmed me. 'I'll be with you just as soon as I

can,' he said. 'By the first available plane to Paris in the morning and then by train.'

The house seemed larger and very still. My legs continued to tremble, but I still felt enveloped in a strange peace. I looked at Matilda, I walked round the foot of the bed, I put on the lamp but I missed the sound of her heavy breathing. I tried to move about noisily. I talked to her in a very loud voice about anything that happened to pass through my mind. I did my best to appear brave, and then suddenly I collapsed over the bed and kissed her desperately, as I had never kissed anybody before. She had already lost some of her living warmth and I knew, coward that I was, that I would soon lose my bravado.

I had left some of the things which I had ironed earlier in the day on the metal covers of the Aga to air. These I now carefully folded and began to put away in a cupboard in her room. I half thought of my mother as being still asleep. I could not accustom myself to the truth.

My hands when accomplishing the most ordinary tasks seemed lighter than usual. They might have been possessed by some spirit. I remembered that I had not closed the stable doors and that my unfortunate hens would be at the mercy of a prowling fox. I had not been out of the house except to meet Patsy. I would have to get used to the idea of going out and finding it empty on my return.

The hens were huddled against one another in what now seemed an enormous space. When they saw me they became petrified, remembering what had happened earlier in the day. Like myself they had received a terrible shock.

Night had not yet fallen and the birds were still singing. But it was very cold, and as I passed through the boiler-room I increased the heat. I switched on the television. Nothing made sense and I switched it off again. At ten o'clock I tuned in to the news from London and the sound of Big Ben was comforting. I made some fresh tea. Though the central heating was full on I was still cold and unbelievably tired. I am not quite sure how this equated with the feeling of peace that persisted in my mind. As I went from room to room, tidying up, putting things away, I found myself unconsciously praying—sometimes silently, at other times aloud. I chiefly thanked God for not allowing me to leave Matilda during her last hours, and most of all for allowing me to be there at the very end. I could so easily have absented myself for a moment, gone out into the kitchen garden to get a lettuce, run out to get a pail of coke for the Aga or some anthracite for the central heating, and on my return I might have found that during those very moments life had left her. That would have weighed on me intolerably. But now my heart was bursting with gratitude and I cried out: 'Merci, merci, mon Dieu!' I filled a pail with soapy water and washed the kitchen floor whose white-and-black tiles were over a hundred years old. Sleep was stealing over me. My body seemed to be floating in space, while my head became heavier, dragging me down. What must I do? I recalled that after the death of my father my mother and I had dragged a mattress on to the tiles of the kitchen floor in our airless apartment at Clichy and that exhausted we had slept soundly in each other's arms, the widow and the orphan.

'There's no sense', said my mother, 'in holding a wake.' These many years afterwards I would remember her words and go upstairs in search of temporary forgetfulness.

I went first into Matilda's room, where I shut off the radiator and closed the window. Then I kissed her and wished her good night—and slowly I left the room. Those wonderful lines which Scarron wrote for his epitaph, and which my mother and I so often repeated to each other, kept on running through my head. After a turbulent and frivolous youth, the author of the *Roman comique* had spent the greater part of his life crippled and tortured by rheumatism. The poet had immortalized his abominable sufferings in these lines which we had first discovered in the *Petit Dictionnaire Larousse* which Matilda gave me when I was a little girl to help me get through my school leaving certificate. At school I had enthused about the poet, hating with equal vigour his wife, Mme de Maintenon, who when she ruled over the heart and conscience of Louis XIV, the Sun King, incited him to revoke the Edict of Nantes which was to bring about the massacre of the Protestants and the exile of so many others. A little girl can get very worked up.

My mother, reading Scarron's epitaph for the first time in Larousse, had said to me: 'My own poor father was crippled and tortured like he was.' We were both sewing, and I saw her put down the book, take up her needle again and I remember being struck by the speed with which her beautiful white hands flew over the material.

Never had I seen such lovely hands. How could I have had any idea that forty years later I would see them twisted into fantastic shapes, robbed of their usefulness, traversed by swollen veins, black as snakes?

Tears ran down my cheeks, I cried as one cries in one's extreme youth. It was as if I were emptying my very soul. But all the time the words of the seventeenth-century poet were running through my brain:

> He who now sleeps here
> Was an object of pity rather than of envy,
> And suffered a thousand deaths
> Before he died.

> Passer-by, do not make any noise here,
> Be very careful not to wake him;
> For this is the first night
> That poor Scarron has been able to sleep.

Of which this is the text in Old French:

> Celui qui cy maintenant dort
> Fit plus de pitié que d'envie,
> Et souffrit mille fois la mort
> Avant que de perdre la vie.
>
> Passant, ne fais ici de bruit
> Garde bien que tu ne l'éveille;
> Car voici la première nuit
> Que le pauvre Scarron sommeille.

I closed my mother's door softly, and, followed by my Pekinese, I went up to my bedroom for the first time in a week and fell fast asleep.

6

I SLEPT the sleep of utter exhaustion and woke up refreshed the next morning to face the first day of my new life as a daughter without a mother. I had, of course, as yet scarcely realized what had happened. The surprise and newness of the situation had made it feel unreal.

On coming downstairs I passed through the living-room, or the low room as we often called it, and paused for a moment on the threshold of the kitchen. My body became of a sudden taut. Then, anxious to prove to myself that I was brave, I went straight to my mother's room and said in a loud voice, 'Good morning, mother. You slept well!' and I kissed her on the forehead. The shock of the marble cold flesh, though expected, was sufficiently violent to upset my calculated poise. I knew at that moment that I would never see her again alive. On the other hand it is only when Death enters the house that one begins to realize the full promise of resurrection. It was at this point that I knew beyond doubt that I believed in an after-life.

I went into the kitchen to fetch some scissors and with these I cut off a lock of her hair. It was the colour of a maple leaf in the fall of the year. Her features were rested and she appeared younger.

Mlle Seguin, the nurse, arrived.

'I've come to say good morning and to help you,' she said. 'I knew yesterday that your dear mother was dying. The injections I gave her were useless, but at least we have the consolation of knowing that she didn't feel them.'

Then came the doctor who, seating himself at the kitchen table, wrote out the certificate, which he sealed before handing it to me. I was to take it to the Mairie. While he was still there the postman arrived with the letters. He said that Mme Thibert when acknowledging receipt for her pension the previous day had signed her name on the wrong line. Would she give him another signature?'

'I'm sorry,' I said, 'but, alas, I can do nothing for you. My mother died at 6.40 last evening.'

'In that case,' he answered, 'forgive me. It doesn't matter.'

The doctor rose from his chair, and while putting away his fountain-pen informed me that he was very tired. After lunch he would be off on his summer holidays. He hoped the weather would be fine. I asked him for his bill. He consulted a small notebook, made a hasty addition and, setting out the total, handed it me politely, but with an air of such frigid correctness that had I not known him better I could have mistaken it for cynicism. His fees were within a franc or two of the money that the postman had brought Matilda the previous day, and I thought with sudden joy of the happiness it would have given her to know that her pension had arrived in time to pay her last debt, and that she would be leaving the world without owing a penny to anybody. She had refused all her life to owe money or to buy anything on credit. This was her credo which she instilled into me.

Thus it was finished. The nurse and the doctor departed, the doctor looking up into the sky to see what the weather portended. His handshake sent a cold tremor down my spine, but at heart I was grateful to him for not having sought to lessen my grief with useless sympathy. It was better as it was.

The twelve-hour strike of electricity and gas from 6 a.m. to 6 p.m. was partly paralysing the life of the nation. The refrigerator was already de-iced, the pumps had ceased to bring water up from the well, everything in the house had come to a halt.

When Georgette arrived she, who when Matilda was alive talked in such a loud voice, spoke only in a whisper. Patsy, who was a model of kindly understanding, relieved me of every official formality. I was afraid to drive, and I noticed that whereas my mind was alert my speech had become incoherent. So I decided not to go down to the village. Longuet, the carpenter, came to tell me that in order to make the coffin while the electricity was still functioning he had worked all through the night. He could now promise it for the morning, and as Thursday was Ascension Day, Matilda would be taken to the twelfth-century church at Auberville tomorrow morning, Wednesday, where the *curé* of Villers would conduct the service.

As soon as I was left alone I threw myself into the most intensive housework, cleaning the kitchen and tidying Matilda's room. I then turned my attention to cupboards and drawers. Matilda's possessions were pathetically few. Also amongst her papers were two death certificates—those of my father, Milou, and of her second husband, Thibert. She had married the first in Paris and the second in London. Amongst her papers also a photograph of herself in 1916 and one of my cousin Rolande and me dressed like twin sisters. There were letters from her grandson when at the age of eight he was making his film *The Fallen Idol*, most of them from Shepperton or from our London flat, but one or two from the Ritz in Paris while he was dubbing the film in French. He described a visit to Versailles and to the Invalides. I closed my eyes and saw again his blond head between my husband and myself at dinner at the Ritz Grill. We had ordered a salad and the *maître d'hôtel* had asked my son very solemnly, as if he were already grown up, if it was to his liking, and the child had answered equally solemnly: 'It is very good but not so good as the ones Granny

makes.' And the *maître d'hôtel* had answered most politely:
'Of that I am very certain, monsieur, for how could anybody make a better salad than a granny?'

So it had always been. No salad was ever so good as
Granny's salads. Nor were any jams so fragrant as hers
which she made with the fruit in the orchard. He would
remember them all his life, as I remembered the gooseberry
jellies which my grandmother at Blois used to make.

There was a special bag which my mother called her
'German Occupation Handbag' because it had remained
with her throughout her difficult war years at Versailles
when she was so unhappily separated from us.

At the bottom of this I found her wedding ring which
Bayard, the local painter, had sawn off her finger when her
hands became crippled with rheumatism. The thin circle of
gold was therefore broken and there was a tiny space
between the two ends. Even so I who pride myself on my
hands could only get it on to my little finger. Consider
therefore how beautiful her hands must once have been.
There was also a ring with a small diamond which I had
given her at the time of my marriage.

I started to make neat piles of her linen and also to put out
her blouses, those lovely blouses she had made herself. Only
last summer she had miraculously managed to make one.
When I was in London I used to search the remnant counter
at Dickins & Jones to find suitable material for her
blouses, for this had been one of her favourite shops, and I
had only to tell her that a piece of material came from there
for my gift to be appreciated. Fifille started to bark joyously,
and on going to the kitchen door I saw Mme Javault
dressed in black, for she was in mourning for her husband
and was on her way to Mass.

'I have come to see my friend,' she said.

After a while the sun came out and we took two kitchen
chairs into the garden. We talked about Matilda, and

suddenly we heard a great buzzing and found ourselves
enveloped in a cloud of bees. Neither of us spoke nor
moved. The loud music they made seemed incredibly peaceful, and I for my part was not at all afraid. The bees so full of
life had come in search of a home. They reminded me of
Milou's hot Midi and of that lovely story by Paul Arène in
which he says that one must always inform the bees of anything important that takes place in one's house, especially
of a birth, a marriage or a death. For some years past the
bees had flown round my house without ever settling there.
What would happen this time? The noise they made was
almost deafening.

After a while the bees moved away and I said to Mme
Javault: 'Is there anything belonging to my mother that
you would like?'

'Mme Henrey,' she answered, 'I also am no longer young
and I own trunkfuls of clothes which I shall never wear,
clothes bequeathed me by my aunts, but all the same
there is something of your Mama's that I would greatly
esteem.'

'What is that, Mme Javault?'

'Her blue aprons. You see, Mme Henrey, we planned
those aprons together. It was I who bought the material in
the market at Villers and I admired your Mama for being
able still to make so many things with her poor twisted
fingers whilst I, whose hands are in no way hurt, am
incapable of making anything at all. Yes, indeed, those
aprons would give me much pleasure, and every time I
wore one I would think of her.'

I went to fetch them.

'Your Mama's death will change my life as well as yours,'
said Mme Javault after a while. 'Twice a week I came here
to see her, and when my dear husband died she was so full
of compassion.'

She had followed me into Matilda's room and stood

silently watching while I kissed my mother. 'The coldness of her forehead frightens me,' I said.

'Yes,' said Mme Javault, 'but it also reassures one. How else would one be quite certain that their souls had departed? Perhaps you would allow me to remain a moment alone with your Mama?'

I went out of the room, closing the door behind me. Did Mme Javault kneel at my mother's bedside and pray a moment? I will never know, but I watched the little figure in black disappear up the orchard path while I remained with my dead mother and the bees.

For the bees had come back and now they were everywhere. They came into the house through all the open windows and some of them were left struggling on the window sills. But I wanted them alive and not dead. I prayed that they would find a home in my house.

At 9 p.m. my husband arrived. Patsy and Jacques had gone to fetch him at the station. He had left London that morning by the first available plane, reaching Le Bourget just after two o'clock. The electricity strike had produced chaos in the capital. The traffic lights had ceased to function, and there was such congestion in the streets that he had been warned at Le Bourget that it might take him several hours to reach the Gare St Lazare where, according to hasty information, there was a train at three-thirty for Deauville.

My telephone call the previous night had caught him as he was about to leave the apartment for a literary party in the West End. He had arranged to meet our son there later in the evening. Had it not been for this he might have crossed on the night boat by Southampton–Le Havre, but he rightly considered it vital to acquaint Bobby with the news of Granny's death. Thus by an unhappy quirk he found himself obliged to do so in an atmosphere of laughter, champagne and caviare.

This party given by a *restaurateur* to launch a new novel by his authoress daughter was in every way sumptuous. For my husband this setting made his anxiety for me all the more poignant. Then, as if to make the night more dark and unforgettable, news came through to him towards 9 p.m. that a great wave of selling had hit Wall Street, producing a slump which was already being likened to that of 1929. The volume of sales was so heavy that the high-speed ticker-tape was swamped, and closing prices were coming in nearly an hour late. Would this foreshadow a tragic repetition of thirty odd years before?

By morning the Wall Street slump had spread to all the capitals of Europe. In Paris as in London prices plunged, and the despondency in Paris was made almost tangible by the effects of the electricity strike that entangled transport, stopped lifts, darkened offices and brought teleprinters to a standstill at the very moment when so much was at stake.

When my husband finally reached the Gare St Lazare he discovered there was no train till six o'clock. Three hours later Patsy and Jacques brought him in their Déesse to my garden gate and then tactfully left us alone. His presence brought me a feeling of intense relief. The electricity was working again, and it was as if a great darkness had lifted from the land. But grief had made me almost unrecognizable and we clung to each other in silence. Then because he had not eaten all day, I cooked some eggs and we sat facing each other at the kitchen table. My husband spoke about things that had happened in London. The sound of his loved voice was sweet to my ears, and a feeling of thankfulness for his safe arrival stole caressingly over me.

I took him to see Matilda. This was the last night she would spend under our roof. When I kissed her I broke down and sobbed. Yet even as my husband and I, hand in hand, went upstairs I began to experience again that wonderful comfort of being two, of having somebody to share my unhappiness, and, with my husband beside me, I fell asleep and to my shame never woke till morning.

That Wednesday morning just as we had sat down to breakfast Longuet and three men arrived with the coffin. My husband implored me to absent myself while he and Longuet performed those last simple acts which are perhaps the most painful for those who remain behind, and, coward that I am, I fled. Shall I for ever regret it? I cannot make up my mind. Perhaps I had reached the end of human endurance.

My mother had asked me to let her remain for a short while in the cottage which adjoins our house and where she had lived at one time. Her coffin was accordingly placed on the oak table made from trees in our woods. Here the coffin was sealed to allow it to pass from one commune to another —from the commune of Villers to that of Auberville. At eleven o'clock Longuet came back with a hearse from Trouville—a motor hearse to replace the one that not so very long ago used to be drawn by a white carthorse owned by a neighbouring farmer. As this motor hearse drove up our orchard my husband and I followed in my little Citroën, I at the wheel, dressed in black with the black stockings that Georgette had bought me and wearing the mantilla that my son had given me on his return from Spain.

The morning was cloudy and cold.

Nothing could be more picturesque than this church of Auberville with its quiet churchyard on a high cliff over-looking the Channel.

Just beyond the lich-gate stood Patsy, her uncle, David Owen, M. Woolf, a neighbour, and Georgette and Jacques, our young farmers. Raiteault and his men lifted the coffin from the hearse, and my husband and I followed it to the church door where the recently installed *curé* of Villers was waiting with two altar boys.

The tiny church, whose roof and spire were russet tiled in the Norman manner, was very quiet. As in our house which Matilda had just left for ever, cross-beams hewn with the axe out of great trees spanned the low roof. The walls were whitewashed, and I had the comfortable sensation of being drawn closer to generations of Norman peasants who, in the days when churches in hamlet or isolated village played a more vital part in community life, drove to Mass in trap or buggy, finding in their simple faith their deepest and most poignant satisfaction.

The heavy oak coffin lay just in front of me under the low blanched beams. The priest's voice was gentle and moving: 'Recevez, Seigneur, votre servante . . .'

These words evoked my mother in the flaming beauty of her youth, simple as she always was, retiring and shy, an apron tied round her slim waist. Yes, a servant wearing an apron and fulfilling a humble but all important role in the heart of her small family, sewing, mending, cooking, never for a moment idle, meek in the presence of my tall father— the strong, wild, impetuous Milou—but quick to defend the little blonde girl who was her daughter.

'Recevez, Seigneur, votre servante . . .'

Before leaving home I had gone out into the garden to pick a posy which now lay, looking very small and humble, on the coffin. It was made up of a single red rose—the only one in bloom—some white pansies and a few forget-me-nots. Round the short stems I had tied the green ribbon which at Easter had encircled the chocolate egg I had bought for her in Bond Street. Bobby had given her this small gift on his arrival, and she had appreciated it all the more because it had come from England. Into the posy also I had stuck a small Union Jack and a Tricolor. Apart from this posy there were no flowers.

When the service was over we went into the churchyard, where the smell of hawthorn sweetened the May morning. Matilda would remain in the little church until after Ascension Day. The mayor of the hamlet introduced himself. He said that we could choose the site of the grave. He was a modest man who had once been a farmer, but now because of the sudden death of his wife was retired. He was so heartbroken that we almost felt as if we were intruding upon his own sorrow, but he very gently helped us choose a plot of grass, explaining the various things we were to do and asking me to call on him at the little house on the main road to Caen which served as the Mairie and which was open on one morning every week.

The hearse had disappeared. The priest had driven off in his car. So had Patsy, David Owen, M. Woolf, Georgette and Jacques—all of them had tactfully slipped away. Now it was the mayor's turn to leave us. Matilda, *servante du Seigneur*, was in the locked church. On this cliff overlooking the Channel her final resting-place was not yet ready to receive her.

Honeysuckle covered the hedges on both sides of the lane which led to the main road. My husband liked me to drive him, and we were almost ashamed of the joy we both felt in being together. Half way home we saw the hearse drawn up in the courtyard of the Café Alleaume. Raiteault and his men would be refreshing themselves inside, and this sudden evocation of the stories of Guy de Maupassant gave me an unpleasant shock. Yet I also felt the urge to seek violent relief from my sorrow. We would go home, collect Fifille and lunch in a restaurant at Trouville. I couldn't face the emptiness of the house, the knowledge that there would be nobody in my mother's room.

So we went to Trouville by the coast road. This seaside

resort has miraculously changed little since I first knew it, and indeed I suppose it is not so very different from what it was when Boudin set up his easel on its magnificent sands. There is still the picturesque fish market on the Trouville bank of the Dives River only a few hundred yards from where the river joins the sea, and on market-days the farmers and market gardeners set up their produce all the way from the fish market to the bridge which links Trouville with Deauville. The Casino, with its ochre façade, imparts a pre-1914 flavour to the landscape, and the steep winding streets leading to the higher part of the town have so far prevented the sort of modernization which could destroy the town's original character. At all events I like it well, and on this unforgettable morning we inquired of one of the fishwives behind her stall which in her opinion was the best small restaurant where we could find a dish of hot mussels and a few early strawberries at this time of year.

She sent us to a small place whose red velvet *banquettes* and Edwardian paintings on the walls gave it an atmosphere reminiscent of the Café Royal before its rebuilding. In short this too was pre-1914. We drank an excellent Burgundy, and though the restaurant was almost empty but for a group of owners and trainers from a neighbouring stud farm, we thought it very gay. But I kept on thinking about the house without Matilda, and how I would no longer see her blanched features pinched with pain as she sat at the kitchen table reading her *Daily Express* or her *Daily Mail*. These came to her every day from London and she read them very thoroughly, comparing their different presentations of the news.

After this lunch—the first time my husband and I had been to a restaurant together for quite a long time—we drove to the Magasins du Printemps at Deauville. This was always a favourite expedition, for the store has a Parisian air about it and one invariably finds there a good deal of what is newest in the capital. There were some very large straw bags for the *plage* in the maddest, gayest colours which I found myself on the point of buying when I suddenly remembered that they could not at this moment be for me. We bought a boat-shaped dish made in Athens and on which was reproduced in Greek lettering a passage from the Epistle of St Paul to the Corinthians which we had found it fun in the shop to decipher and recognize. The afternoon had turned very cold and by tea time we were back at the farm.

The warmth of the Aga welcomed us. Matilda was no longer there, but in a way, and I am almost ashamed to write it, the queen was dead, long live the queen. For it was as if the house had suddenly become mine, and during the next few days, before my husband was obliged to return to London, we found ourselves planning certain changes. I would, for instance, entirely redecorate Matilda's room and turn it into a sewing-room for myself. I had never owned, either in London or in the country, what my mother-in-law had called a 'little' room, a room in which I could spread out my own belongings and sew or rest in the afternoons. I had suddenly tired of painted walls and chose instead a very gay wallpaper with clusters of roses which when put up made the room appear like a bandbox from a smart milliner's shop.

Alas—I say it again—my husband and I were at times deliriously happy, as if we had emerged from some long, dark tunnel to find liberty and sunshine. Yes, the house was ours. We could be as noisy as we liked, and this was a thing which hitherto had been impossible, impossible ever since we had first bought the place. Indeed even now there were moments when we forgot that we were alone and, because it was engrained in us, we talked in a whisper not to disturb Matilda who might be resting or in pain. We could go out driving in the country or sunbathing on the sands and come back when we liked without telling ourselves that we must be back at some special hour because of a set meal. We could lunch or dine at any time we liked—or if we felt like it not at all.

As the time approached for my husband to return to London, the old fear which his presence had momentarily quelled came over me again, disturbing my nights. My mother still lay in her coffin in the church at Auberville, and it now seemed probable that I would find myself alone at the graveside when she was lowered to her final resting place.

My husband was taking the night boat by Le Havre. At about four o'clock in the afternoon, when he was at the bottom of the orchard inspecting some young apple trees, I heard the tinkling of the Austrian cowbell at our garden gate. It was Longuet, who had come to help me move my mother's old Norman cupboard from what had been her room to one of the bedrooms upstairs, and to tell me that the gravedigger had now done his work and that the burial was to take place within half an hour. He would be going there himself to help.

This news brought me great relief. My husband had already packed his bags, and now only needed to put on a dark suit in which he would travel.

The church when we reached it was open and a ray of warm sunshine illuminated the stained-glass window enveloping the coffin in rainbow colours. I knelt down and kissed her lips through the wood as I had seen a Russian friend do at the Orthodox church in London. My little bouquet was still fresh and I took it with me to throw into the grave.

Our little procession moved off very slowly. The coffin was extremely heavy, and Longuet had only recently recovered from a serious abdominal operation, so that my husband and the gravedigger did their best to take more than their share of the weight. The grave surprised me by its depth, and I was now able to understand why my farmer, Jacques, had been asked to bring a cart to remove the surplus earth. Longuet and his companion slipped the ropes into place, and slowly lowered the coffin. I threw my little bouquet down—and it was all over. Irrevocably over.

But at least my husband and I had been together for this final parting. We had prayed together, held hands and shared our grief. I felt stronger to face what the future might hold in store.

7

THAT night was the first I had passed alone in my domain.

The kitchen was warm and well lit, and for company I had a choice of television or sound radio. The advantages I now enjoyed made the days of my childhood seem too remote to be real. Those long evenings when my mother sewed painfully under the lamp in our flat in Clichy, my father's anxiety when in bad weather men were laid off in the building trade, my poor mother's valiant efforts to find enough money to buy her little girl a pair of shoes, my frivolous Aunt Marie-Thérèse's penny novelettes—what a great space of time divided me from memories such as these! I doubt if I could even write *The Little Madeleine* today. A Parisian journalist once interviewed me about my girlhood in a television programme, and he attacked me almost savagely for having painted so dramatic a picture of poverty. He was annoyed that the book had made such an impression in England and in America. He felt that I had discredited the country of my birth. How could I explain that the facts I had set down were scrupulously accurate and that I have a horror of exaggeration in any form? His incredulity was excusable. There is no picturesque poverty left and my interviewer was too young to have known the Montmartre of my youth, the Montmartre of Picasso and the Impressionists.

'And yet', I had exclaimed in an effort to convince him, 'Oliver Twist was far more unhappy than I was, and the poverty that Dickens described was vast.'

166

'Yes, of course,' he countered, 'but that was not in 1912!'

But in fact the difference between the days that Dickens described and 1912 was far less marked than between 1912 and today. Matilda represented the generation of women who had witnessed the greatest change in their standard of living.

If I had been given the talent to paint not in words but on canvas youthful Matilda with her mass of copper-coloured hair, her slim waist and ankle-length skirts going off on a Sunday morning to wash her linen at the *lavoir*, she would not be forgotten, as perhaps she will be, but immortalized. Why did I not have the gift of a Douanier Rousseau to paint La Mère Gontrel with Riri in her arms as she set off from our street to sing her ballads in the courtyards of rich houses in the XVIth arrondissement? No wonder that the canvases of the French Impressionists are sold at ever-increasing prices. The picturesque poverty of their surroundings—the surroundings in which Matilda passed her early married life —has disappeared for ever. This is the age of television.

On Thursday morning I went as I had promised to the Mairie of Auberville to sign various documents concerning my mother's grave. The Mairie consisted of little more than one room containing the bust of the republic, a cupboard for the archives and a large table. A new floor was being laid and in a corner of the room, the old floor having been taken up and the new one not yet having been put down, one could see the very earth upon which this small house was built. The bust of Marianne with her revolutionary cap made me think of the various Scarlet Pimpernels of the period, and seeing these foundations laid bare I realized how easily in these old houses one could hide documents, valuables or even a person under the floor of the most honest-looking Mairie.

On this June morning M. le Maire and his assistant were seated at the table. The assistant was writing the details concerning my case slowly and in a fine hand with a ball-point pen. The decorative inkpot looked as if it dated from the days of quills and was dry of ink. 'You sign here,' he said, handing me his pen, 'where it says "Daughter of the deceased". It will be your duty to tend the grave in perpetuity.'

The mayor and his assistant rose and shook me by the hand. Midday was about to strike and the Mairie would be closing till the following Thursday.

As the weather became warmer the summer visitors began to arrive, and I found myself drawn into that circle of young mothers and children who every year descended upon Jacques and Patsy at Montauzan.

The violent contrast between what I had gone through during the last few weeks and this effervescence of young life left me at first a little dazed. Montauzan, in spite of the presence of Mrs Owen, had never been gayer. Besides, there was nothing austere or forbidding in this smiling grandmother who remained like a figure in a Victorian story book reading or laboriously trying to do some tapestry in a corner of the big room where the family and their guests came in and out making all the noise they pleased.

Patsy, meeting me in the village one morning, exclaimed: 'Jacqueline's arrived! You'll find her in front of our bathing tent on the beach.'

Jacqueline was a Gaudin. All the members of this distinguished family were musical and my readers will remember them in *Mistress of Myself*. Jacqueline's brother Daniel, an actor and producer, was married to the beautiful Natalie, a ballet dancer. Her sister Marie-Christine was a violinist, who while her husband was called up played in the philharmonic orchestra in Paris. Jacqueline herself and her young husband Guy made documentary films, which did not prevent Jacqueline from being an enthusiastic mother who already had three children, two boys and a baby girl. All had acquired, through stage and film and much travelling, the imperviousness of the strolling player to his surroundings. As soon as they arrived in a strange place they unpacked their things, put an alarm clock by the bed to wake them in time for the next rehearsal, and all was well. Nearly all the young women in this set had university degrees and a rather better acquaintance with Latin and Greek than most men, and yet they all refused to part with their children, whom they brought up without paid help or nannies.

I discovered Jacqueline, as Patsy had told me I would, on the sands in front of the Poirots' bathing tent. This was our special place and in the summer we all came here—Dr Lehérissey and his wife, the two Drs Durville (father and son) and their families, Jacques and Patsy, their children and all their guests. Even in August when the trippers arrived, the summer residents—families that remained at Villers throughout the summer—never seemed to get ousted from their privileged spots.

Jacqueline was demurely knitting, though I could see that her mind was on her children who were making sand castles. There was little Charles, who was the eldest, Pascal, very serious for his three years, and the baby daughter who put her little arms round her mother's neck at the slightest provocation. 'And I'm expecting another,' said Jacqueline with obvious satisfaction.

She was so at peace with the world and so happy with her children that it was amusing to reflect how well ordered had become the lives of the modern equivalent of the strolling players of Théophile Gautier's day. Theatre people were no longer improvident. Perhaps the tax collector had something to do with it. Most of them dreamed of buying an apartment in Paris, an extremely costly undertaking. When at the end of the month they had put aside the money for the mortgage and enough to pay for food and clothes, there was little left over for that riotous living which so many people associate with their profession.

The apartment that Jacqueline and her husband had bought was just outside Paris, and there was one garden for all the tenants—or should one say for all the co-owners?—but from what Jacqueline said it seemed to work well.

'One just has to get on well with neighbours in the same building,' she explained, 'for one is virtually saddled with them for life. When you're buying a flat for ten thousand pounds you can't very well pack up and go elsewhere. Nor can the others. So the best thing is to learn how to make friends. "The goat must browse where it's tethered," says the proverb. What is, is!'

She and her husband were extremely religious. At the beginning of their married life, before their first child, they had gone to Portugal to make a documentary at Notre Dame de Fatima, and they had come back touched by faith. Was it already dormant within them, and had this experience served to waken it? At all events it had greatly increased their love for each other, and they now radiated a serenity in which their cleverness and wit crackled like popcorn. As for Jacqueline, whether she was in skin-tight jeans or in a bikini, her happiness was made up of the nicest things in life.

She had in addition to Daniel, Natalie's husband, another brother called Marcel, also an actor, who was camping under an orange-coloured tent on the lawns of Montauzan. He had just returned from Algeria where he had done two years' military service. Of this he was far from proud. The experience might have been rewarding, he claimed, if it had not been for the futility of army life which had prevented him from gaining any advantage from what might have been an instructive journey.

'Of course,' he added, with the dry Gaudin wit, 'two years of arrested growth are not without compensation for those of us who are intellectuals, for they retard the moment when too much erudition turns us into lunatics.'

He had a very pretty gift for reciting the sonnets of Shakespeare and whole poems of Robert Burns. We all used to listen entranced while his sister continued with incredible patience to look after her children, laying down her knitting to hunt for a lost spade, to take a pullover off Charles or to put one on his brother.

Patsy meanwhile was eternally worried about her eldest son. Would he, or would he not, pass his examinations? Bunny, as she called him, dazzled us by his scientific knowledge. At other times, in spite of his seventeen years, he seemed a real baby. He had lately begun to smoke, and though he did not appear to enjoy it, his parents, I think, felt that it made him look manly.

One evening at low tide we were all on the sands when Bunny came back from his first day's papers. He told us some of the questions and, turning to his mother, gave her a brief outline of his answers. Patsy, a bluestocking, and a great admirer of Simone de Beauvoir, discoursed brilliantly on what her son should have done, and ended by exclaiming: 'My poor child, I am much afraid that you'll be ploughed.' The same thing happened the next evening. A fortnight later, however, she telephoned from Montauzan with the news that he had passed his *baccalaureat*. The family honour was saved.

Titine Bayard, that fine portly woman with the neat bun on top of her head, who for so long helped me with my housework, had been a good friend of my mother's, and I reflected that it would be nice to offer her one or two of my mother's things.

Bayard, Titine's husband, was a house painter, and many was the time that he had been sent by Barbe, the contractor, to paint my house. Husband and wife were hard-working and scupulously honest. For many years they had put money aside to give their son a chance to better himself. He had indeed become a schoolmaster with an assured future. Now that this dream was realized the Bayards decided to build a house of their own where they could spend a happy retirement. The government had a scheme by which it helped artisans to do this. Bayard built his every evening after his painting work was done. Unfortunately the day it was finished he fell ill and nearly died. The effort had proved too much.

Still, they had the house, and though Bayard must take things very easily, hardly walking, being careful not to lift anything at all heavy, they were not faced with any more financial worries, because every summer they could live in a tiny flat at the back of the house and let all the rest of it to holiday makers for enough money to meet their needs during the entire year. Titine occasionally supplemented this income by making mattresses or recarding the wool in old ones.

I found her in the shed where she kept her old-fashioned carding machine, whose jaws bristled with spikes to comb the wool and make it soft. She was not pleased with me, she said, because I had not told her about my mother's death. Did we no longer consider her a friend? She was not the only one, she added, to feel this way. The entire village was a little hurt that the service at Auberville had been kept secret. Was it because nobody could quite make out whether we were Catholics or Protestants?

I told her that my mother had died in the faith in which she was born. She was a Roman Catholic and had been to a convent at Blois. I did not think it necessary to add that the extreme poverty she had known as a young woman in Paris, the cruel loss of her baby son and recently her years of abominable suffering had embittered her to the point where she had ceased to believe in anything. She was of the opinion that from the day of her birth she had been under a malediction. She was not the first to ask herself if certain people are not made without any apparent reason to atone during their sojourn on earth for the sins of past genera- tions. There was so little explanation otherwise for the ill fortune which had attended her from her earliest and most tender years.

That our family had divided loyalties in religion while remaining fundamentally united in the love of Christ was as puzzling to certain of our friends as that we had two countries and two languages. What made it more confusing, almost as confusing to us as it was to them, was that we were so perfectly at home in each. There were moments when we ceased to be aware of what language we were speaking, and we prayed as humbly in one church as in another.

Nevertheless the new *curé* of Villers had thought it wise to send me an emissary to inquire about my mother before agreeing to conduct the service. This I did not tell Titine.

She said: 'I must tell you the manner of my hearing the news. It so happened that on Sunday, which you will recall was Mothers' Sunday, my son Jean-Louis, the schoolmaster, sent word that he would be coming to see me with his wife and two children. Wishing to look my best to receive them, I opened my cupboard and took out some sheer stockings, an absolutely new pair from England which Mme Thibert had given me. "I'm going to wear the stockings Mme Thibert gave me," I called out to Bayard. "You see if I don't have news of her before long!" And indeed I didn't have to wait long, for on the Wednesday morning, as I was turning the corner to call at the milk shop, I saw Longuet and his men placing a coffin on his lorry.

'"Who is dead?" I asked.

'"Somebody you knew very well," he answered, "Mme Henrey's mother, and we are burying her today at Auberville!"'

Titine paused because M. le Curé, who had been passing along the street, had heard her voice and, as he was looking for somebody whose house he could not find, he entered the shed.

'Madame,' he said to Titine, 'as I am new here I haven't yet had enough time to call on all my parishioners. I wonder if you could direct me to the house I am looking for?'

Titine, who knew everybody in the village, gave him the information he desired. M. le Curé thanked her, said a few words to me—for had he not come to my help in tragic circumstances?—and went on his way.

Henriette, Titine's sister, who had been sitting quietly in a corner, now started to tell me about her son Raymond who had died soon after his return home from Algiers, where he had been doing his military service. He had caught tuberculosis. She could not get over her loss.

During the Whitsun holiday my friend Yolande arrived with her husband, Paul Huet. Yolande is a tall, slim blonde. In the street men turn round to take a second look at her. She has that indefinable quality known as sex appeal.

Parisian friends of theirs, she told me, had just bought a tiny house facing the sea at Blonville for which they had paid little more than five hundred pounds.

'Can't you find us one like it?' she implored me. 'The smallest house ever built with a balcony on which one can sew, knit, sunbathe, shell peas and take all one's meals! It wouldn't be too far from Paris or London and I could live in jeans and a sweater. Or practically naked if it was hot. And before breakfast I could run down to the sea across the wet sand and bathe. And we could go shrimping and go to the village to buy long loaves of hot bread. All our friends could come and see us. They would sleep on the floor, on the balcony, in the garden, anywhere.'

Yolande was standing by the kitchen door, which as usual was open so that she was half in the kitchen, half in the garden, and the sun was playing on her platinum hair. She was dreaming the dream we all dream. Paul had taken a pitcher and in a few moments he would be back with the cider for lunch. We kept it in a building that had once— several hundred years ago—been a bakery at the end of the garden. He knew where everything was, for they often came to stay with me, and when his mother died and his father couldn't bear to be alone, Yolande and Paul had brought him here so that he wouldn't brood.

'Now we want to console *you*,' Yolande had exclaimed on their arrival.

The wind in the orchard had blown her hair about, but she had put it back in place expertly. She knew all the best hairdressers in Paris and in London, and changed her hair styles so often that I could not keep up with them. Everything about her, in fact, was volatile. Her laughter changed to tears without warning, a tragic narration would be brusquely held up to allow her to lament the inadequacies of a new lipstick. She was never without an enormous handbag in which amongst a thousand other things she carried a large mirror of a kind that according to her did not lie. Every time she looked into it she invariably cried out 'Oh, what a face!' though countless women would have given much to possess features half as attractive as hers. She and Paul did their best to tempt me out to dinner, but I would not have made good company. Time must heal the wound, I told them. The river must run its course, as Paloma used to say.

The little room which had been my mother's and was now mine looked so different with its rose-papered walls that it had assumed an entirely new personality. Less than a month ago I had witnessed here the drama of my mother's death, but the room into which I liked to come to sew or to rest bore no relation to the one in which I had held her hand and kissed her forehead during those poignant hours. They were like two different stage sets in a play. One followed the other without the first becoming in any sense blurred or forgotten.

My Swiss sewing-machine was at last ideally placed, and the walnut table in the centre of the room was what I had always wanted for cutting out material when I was planning a blouse or a dress. Now there were flowers in the garden and I filled my room with peonies and early roses which I put into Lalique cut-glass vases that during the first years of my marriage I had given to my mother-in-law and which reverted to me after her death. On a couch I had put a great number of Scotch plaids. I had once seen this done at Gstaad in a chalet where Elsa Schiaparelli and her daughter were staying. In short my room was full of memories which made small objects become precious.

The swarm of bees that had arrived like a cloud in my garden had found a home under the slates. They were level with the head of my bed, and when I put an ear against the wall I could hear a great commotion as they busied themselves in the hive. Their presence so close to me helped me to sleep, and in the day-time they quickly got used to my presence in the garden. I eagerly looked forward to the lavender bushes all round the rose beds coming into bloom.

The bees never came into my bedroom, and yet one day I found honey in a box in which I kept a pale blue chiffon sari and a gold coin a friend gave me on her return from Mecca.

Georgette looked harassed when she brought the milk. She had promised to give Brigitte a shampoo, and was hurrying back to Berlequet to heat a tub of water. I said that I could very well pick Brigitte up after school, give her the shampoo myself and make her sit in the garden to dry her hair in the sun.

'That would be wonderful!' exclaimed Georgette, 'and I can put in an hour on the white-and-yellow gingham dress I'm making for her. Every time I try to get down to it I'm called out to look after the animals.'

I arrived in the village with twenty minutes to spare, so I decided to call in on Mme Alin who keeps the haberdasher's for a pair of scissors. I found her trying to make room for a new consignment of goods destined for the summer residents. The names of new fibres confused her. Everybody knew what nylon was, but there were banlon and crylon and many others, and who could tell what would be invented next?

'But I simply have to keep abreast,' she said. 'I must say to a customer in a firm voice: "This Madame—or Mademoiselle—is banlon!" And I must make the customer realize from the tone of my voice that what I am trying to sell her is especially fine and supple. For if I didn't believe in it why should she?'

I love Mme Alin's *mercerie*. There is a little of everything —silks and cottons, needles and pins, knitting wool, elastic by the yard, the latest bras, slips and briefs, scent, hairpins, buttons and thimbles. In winter she heats her shop with a big brown stove in which she burns apple logs that give a lovely warm smell. I go to her for so many things that I just can't imagine how I could do without her. Sometimes when I have been away for a few weeks I find myself exclaiming: 'Oh, I do hope nothing has happened to Mme Alin's shop!' I am so terribly afraid that one day it will be replaced by something more modern. Mme Alin's *mercerie* is rather like the sewing-room in a convent, a diminutive House of Béguines, what Zizi Jeanmaire would call a '*truc de femmes*', a place for women to forgather. The knitting wools have names like 'The Wool of the Good Shepherd' or 'Grandmother's Wool', and then there were soft white wools from the plains of Caen. I bought my scissors and also a piece of canvas, a few ounces of wool and a blunt needle to teach Brigitte, just in case she didn't know, how to do cross-stitch. That might help to keep her quiet while her hair dried in the sun.

I called next on Mme Desloges, the ironmonger, whose daughter had left the village to get married.

'When my husband was a prisoner of war she proved a wonderful companion,' said Mme Desloges, 'so quick and intelligent. Afterwards, when things began to reappear in the shops for the first time, I had the joy of seeing her surprise. So many of the things that we had taken for granted before the war were quite new—and almost miraculous—for her. One afternoon, for instance, I sent her to the pastrycook's to buy a dessert. She came running back, breathless with excitement: "Mother, I've seen, I've seen"—she could hardly speak—"the most wonderful thing!" She stood in front of me trying to explain exactly what it was. When at last I understood I answered curtly: "A chocolate éclair! Is that what you've seen? Well, what's so wonderful about that?" Her poor face fell. All the joy went out of her. My lack of understanding had deflated her enthusiasm.'

Mme Desloges is a fine woman. Her figure has generous curves. Her smile is large and warm.

'Only the other day', she exclaimed, 'I said to my husband: "Do you realize you've married a Renoir"!'

Why, yes, Mme Desloges could step straight out of a

painting by Renoir. When one sees the fabulous prices that
men are willing to pay for the work of the French Impressionists, one is surprised that their ideas of feminine beauty
should be so out of fashion. Not that Mme Desloges has any
desire to change. Her dark eyes lit up with laughter. She
obviously liked the idea of being a Renoir at the cash desk.

I sat in my small car outside the village school. The clock
struck four, there was a rush of children and a little girl
wearing a blue woollen hood with a satchel in her hand
came running towards me. Her cheeks were red with joy at
the thought that I was waiting in the car for her. As she
opened the door her eyes were level with mine. Throwing
her satchel on the back seat, she stroked Fifille and sat down
beside me.

'How's mother?' she asked. 'Have you seen her?'

She looked up at me so eagerly that I smiled.

'Didn't you go home for lunch?' I asked.

'Yes, of course.'

'Wasn't mother there?'

'Naturally she was there.' But how long three hours can
seem when daughter is separated from mother! 'Have you
seen her? How is she?' Brigitte repeated.

'I saw her leading a cow down our lane,' I said.

'Which one?' asked Brigitte quickly. 'The one with the
white marks on her face?'

'I don't know,' I said. 'I find it terribly difficult to
distinguish one cow from the other.'

'But they are all quite different,' said Brigitte with a note
of exasperation in her voice. 'I suppose it must be the one
for which you telephoned for the inseminator.' I had so
little expected this word in the child's mouth that I gave
quite a start. After all Brigitte was only seven. 'I do hope it
arrived in time!' she said.

'What do you mean?'

'The inseminator,' she explained seriously and patiently, as if I were the little girl and she the grown woman. 'If the inseminator doesn't arrive when the cow needs it, well . . .' Here Brigitte made an eloquent gesture with her hand. 'Well, you understand,' she went on, 'one has to wait another three weeks—and that's a whole month wasted before the heifer arrives.' She seemed very pleased with this *exposé* and added: 'You know now why I was so anxious for news about mother.'

I felt very small, very stupid. This explanation of how life is transmitted with the help of a syringe, so perfectly natural to Brigitte, shocked me. But my little companion was already thinking about something else. What would I give her to eat? Would we call at the pastrycook's? Would we have a game of snakes and ladders?

As we began the steep climb home we stopped from time to time to pick up other little girls—the small daughters of neighbouring farmers. We put off the last of these at the Poulin farm, and were soon in the gay kitchen in front of the warm Aga, getting everything ready for the shampoo. The hot water in the taps was brought up electrically from the well, but the hot-water reserve in the Aga was rain water and this was what we used. When I had washed and set her hair we went out into the garden to have tea and play draughts. Everything that had happened at school that day was told me in detail. Also that she had lost a tooth.

'I shall put it under my pillow tonight, and tomorrow I shall get a present. I took great care not to lose it. Would you like to see it?'

'Not particularly.' Her face fell and, remembering what Mme Desloges had told me about her daughter, I changed my mind and added: 'Yes, I think I would like to see it, very much.'

She was delighted and began to delve into the pockets of

her apron, finally discovering the trophy which she held up
for me to inspect. By six o'clock her hair was dry and I
drove her up the lane to Berlequet. Outside the main gate
she hardly waited for me to stop, but opening the door of
the car sprang out and rushed across the farmyard, scatter-
ing the hens and the geese, and the next moment she had
rushed into the farmhouse. I heard her shrill voice crying
out: 'Mother! Mother!' Nobody else in the world mattered
any longer. How well I understood this impatience, this
slight fear that the house might be empty, that her mother
would not be there waiting for her. Had I not at her age
always run home from school, tortured by the fear that
something might have happened to prevent me from throwing myself into Matilda's outstretched arms?

But Matilda's room, which was mine now, was, alas,
empty and still. Nevertheless in the evening light it looked
lovely and there were roses everywhere. Roses on the walls,
roses in the cut-glass vases and bowls which stood on
embroidered doilies all of the same design.

Returning home on a cruising liner from the West Indies
we had spent a few hours at Madeira. Friends had taken me
to the casino. Though it was late at night we were surrounded on the quayside by the usual crowd of dark-eyed
little boys trying to sell us something. I bought a beautifully
embroidered tablecloth, and my companions laughed at me
because it never occurred to me to haggle over the price. I
paid the full amount. My fellow passengers said: 'You're a
greenhorn. You should have beaten him down!' The
trouble was that I had embroidered since I was a little girl,
and I knew better than my fellow passengers what hours
and hours of work this tablecloth must have represented.
Between experts one doesn't feel like haggling. Besides, the
woman who so laboriously made my tablecloth might have

been ill or half blind. She deserved all she could get. Well, we were just getting into the motor-boat to go out to the liner, when the dark-eyed boy who had sold me the table-cloth came running after me.

'Miss! Miss!' he cried. 'Gift for you!'

He pressed into my hand six organdie doilies, all having the same embroidered design. Did he want to match my generosity? Was it a superb gesture of Latin pride?

The tablecloth and the doilies disappeared when my house was pillaged during the war, but I had kept a pattern of the design on the doilies; and when the sun came out I would sit out in the garden in front of the kitchen door and reproduce very exactly the doilies the dark-eyed boy had so gallantly pressed into my hand.

8

WHEN that morning I answered the telephone, whose strident ringing had shattered the still, cool atmosphere of the old house, I was greeted by my glamorous friend Yolande. In a voice of high-pitched enthusiasm she informed me that she was staying in a room overlooking the sea at the neighbouring resort of Blonville. She had gone back to Paris with her husband, then decided to return for a few nights alone. She had arrived the previous evening.

'A marvellous journey at the wheel of my own car!' she exclaimed. 'Driving like the wind with nobody to tell me to be careful. That's freedom for a girl!' Her happy laugh was clear and triumphant. 'Come and join me. You can leave your car in front of the hotel. There's a cold nip in the air, but it's low tide and we can bury our noses in the warm sand.'

Why indeed should I not go? I too was as free as the elements, mistress of my house, able to go where I liked in my small car. I need no longer feel guilty about going off to enjoy myself while Matilda lunched alone at the corner of the kitchen table. And on my return, supposing I were to arrive back late, I would not have to face that look of reproach which used to chill me and make me search my brain for some scandal, some piece of gossip, which would interest her, and prevent her from thinking about the brief happiness I had enjoyed.

I put on a bathing-costume, over it a jumper and a white

skirt, left my house cheerful and tidy, the Aga radiating a pleasant warmth, the only thing that in my absence seemed alive now, and, calling Fifille, jumped into my car.

The hotel which Yolande had discovered was a converted villa built on the dunes. At high tide the sea lapped against its garden wall. A Parisian woman had fallen in love with it, and in turning it into a small hotel had been careful to retain much of its original Edwardian character. Yolande's attic room had such a wonderful view of the sea that one had the impression of being in a yacht. I found her standing in front of a full-length mirror twisting a square of white chiffon over her complicated hair-do to form a turban.

'The waves!' she exclaimed dramatically. 'They made such a pounding all night that I thought I would never get to sleep.'

She turned her large eyes upon me, and it struck me that I had never seen her so rested or so well.

We lay on the sands getting brown until lunch time. Her transistor played hot music, but when our conversation became particularly enthralling we turned it off momentarily. What more could we desire? We passed in critical review a great number of our feminine acquaintances in Paris, especially those of whom we were jealous. When these discussions had made us sufficiently hungry we lunched at her hotel, very soberly drinking Evian water. We would have liked to share a bottle of Bordeaux, but we were aware that it would have brought a flush to our cheeks and done no good to our figures. We then went to Deauville in Yolande's Dauphine to inspect the smart crowd at the Bar du Soleil, and to see what was new at the Printemps, where the prettiest beach fashions from Paris, Florence and Hollywood were always to be found.

Yolande tried on straw hats, and the more comical ones put us in high good humour. Our laughter was so real that

people turned to look at us, and the shop girls did not hide
their admiration for Yolande's tall, willowy beauty. I wanted
some tailored slacks, and she helped me to choose some
which I took such a liking to that I kept them on. We went
gaily out of the store into the tree-lined streets. Was it
possible that only a few weeks had gone by since I had cried
my eyes out?

The next day I went down to the village to call at the
carpenter's shop. I called at the workroom first in the hope
of finding Longuet, but he was away. A window of the villa
was thrown up and Mme Fanneau, his mother-in-law,
not recognizing me, asked me rather coolly what I
wanted. I explained that her son-in-law was not in the
workroom, but I wondered if her daughter happened to be
at home.

I found Mme Longuet behind a carpet sweeper in the
living-room. The noise it made had doubtless prevented her
from hearing me.

'I've brought you the money for Mother's coffin,' I said.

She put the money in a drawer of the sideboard and said:
'I'm quite worn out. Mother never believes me when I tell
her that I'm tired. She's as strong as a mountain.'

I thought back to a certain day at the beginning of the
war when we were walking back along the powdery road
from the cemetery after the funeral of Nénette Poulin, who
had hanged herself on that historic sunny day when the
Germans had invaded Belgium. The bridges across the
Meuse had been blown up and enemy tanks were streaming
across north-eastern France. The gardens were full of roses
and the produce in our market-places had never been richer.

How could one believe that the world we had known was
coming to an end?

Mme Fanneau, who was walking beside me, said: 'The

hour is very grave. My son and my son-in-law are both at the front and I am without news of them.'

Mme Fanneau was at that time one of the most beautiful women in the village, and yet—it hardly seems credible— she was already a grandmother. But yes, she was truly beautiful! Always so smartly turned out, her hair done in the latest fashion!

She had not recognized me today. I had now reached the age that she was when we had walked back from Nénette's funeral. Her son, Fernand, was deported to a German camp. He died in captivity. Her son-in-law, Longuet, being a carpenter by trade, was put to work in a furniture factory, which was soon turned over to making coffins for the Germans.

One day when he had come to see me at the farm he said to me, leaning over the garden fence: 'Coffins! I scarcely had time to eat or to sleep. As the months went by and to the allied bombardments on German cities were added the mounting casualties on the Russian front we almost dropped at our lathes. But for prisoners like myself who were not allowed to see a newspaper, even if we had been able to understand it, or to listen to the radio, this at least gave us an inkling of what was happening. We occasionally had the impression that we would end by making coffins for the entire German nation.'

At home I still had a lot to do, and sometimes, when I tidied a cupboard or emptied a drawer, I would come across an envelope on which Matilda had written something in her neat hand. There was one which said 'Parsley seeds', and that was enough to bring back all my sorrow and make me cry.

The running of this house immediately after the war had fallen almost entirely on her tired shoulders. She was the first to come back to it after the liberation. The journey from Paris had been worse than a nightmare. She had reached Lisieux at nightfall. The town had been reduced to rubble. Not a house was left standing. Only the great white basilica of Sainte-Thérèse stood unscathed above the ruins. She had spent the night on a kitchen chair, faint with the lack of food and half frozen. And then, of course, when finally she reached the farm, it had been ransacked and she was met by hatred.

There were times when we became a little tired of hearing Matilda's stories about her suffering. They came up regularly like the tales my father Milou told about his army days. They were apt to become a bore. My lack of sympathy now shamed me—so often when she needed me I had abandoned her.

The next day, when Georgette brought me the milk and some green peas from her garden, she said that her uncle had died and that she would have to go to the funeral. She was wondering what to do with Brigitte.

'Would she like to spend the day with me?'

Georgette's features lit up. 'I didn't dare ask you!' she said.

Brigitte arrived with her cross-stitch before nine. I was sitting up in bed writing on a foolscap pad. That was the way I invariably worked with Fifille beside me and all my books and papers spread out on the counterpane. Brigitte was accustomed to seeing me thus and, hoisting herself up on the bed, sat beside me with her little legs stretched out, and it was then that I noticed that she was wearing little wooden mules with miniature high heels.

'I saw them in the market,' she explained, blushing with pleasure. 'Mother didn't want to buy them for me but I told her she could use my savings. They cost seven hundred francs.'

'How did you manage to put so much money aside?'

'Oh, I'm careful,' said this little girl of seven with surprising self-possession. 'When I carry milk or vegetables to mother's customers, they mostly give me fifty francs or twenty francs, and *you* often give me a hundred. So on market-days I can buy small things that take my fancy without having to ask mother for money. But these are the first shoes I've ever bought. It's time, don't you think, that I should have my first high-heeled shoes?'

She was already the little woman, and having delivered her speech busied herself with her cross-stitch while my pen travelled smoothly over the foolscap page. Fifille slept happily between us, her head between her paws. But after a while my companion became restless, and as I had worked well I suggested that we should jump into the car and run down to the sands. We smoothed the counterpane and I tidied her hair. There was a saying that Matilda had picked up when she was a little girl at Blois:

> Le lit fait
> La femme coiffée
> On ne sait pas depuis quand elle est levée.

Which means that when the bed is made, and the woman has done her hair, nobody can tell at what hour she got up. Matilda taught it to me and I taught it to Brigitte.

As it was a fine day and most of the summer residents had arrived, the market-place was colourful and rich in produce. We bought several slices of ham, a piece of Gruyère cheese, two cherry tartlets, some peaches and a yard-long loaf of crisp French bread. Brigitte's eyes shone with pleasure. After a dip in the sea we lay on the sand protected from the wind by a coloured parasol and started our picnic. Natalie Durville, who only a little while ago was still a baby, arrived.

'What are you doing?' she asked in her already impeccable

French. 'A picnic?' But before we had time to answer she saw Brigitte's shoes and, overcome by admiration and envy, exclaimed: 'Shoes with high heels! Oh, oh, will you lend them to me?'

Brigitte looked up at Natalie and did not dare refuse. She was conscious that though they spoke the same tongue their manner of speaking it was different. Natalie, without waiting for an answer, had put on the shoes, and though the heels sank into the dry sand she was filled with delight.

Presently Natalie asked: 'Where did you buy them?'

'In the market-place,' said Brigitte bashfully.

'I'd love to have a pair just like them!'

'Then why don't you ask your mother?' said Brigitte, growing bolder.

'Mama is in Paris,' said Natalie.

Lily Durville, whom readers will have met in *Mistress of Myself*, had four daughters whom we called the 'Little Women'—France, Martine, Sophie and Natalie. At that time France and Martine were strikingly beautiful teenagers, Sophie wore pigtails and Natalie was just learning to walk. Lily Durville, then only thirty-six, used to wear very pretty drain-pipe jeans which accentuated her tiny waist, her narrow hips and youthful breasts, miraculous in a mother of four children.

Four years had gone by. France and Martine were married on the same day. France had a baby boy. Martine was expecting her second child. Lily, not quite forty, was the youngest grandmother I ever met. Just now she was in Paris with Martine waiting for the new baby.

Sophie came to join us. Her long pigtails had been cut off and she was already beginning to look grown up. She and Natalie were being looked after during their mother's absence by Tara, a really beautiful Dutch girl who was with

the family *au pair*. Before they left for lunch I told Natalie
that if I saw some shoes like Brigitte's in the market I would
buy them for her.

Lily Durville came back from Paris that same evening,
though I did not see her until the next day when I went
down to the *plage* as usual. She looked extremely elegant in
bright red tailored slacks and a black jumper. She had
become a grandmother once again—her newest grandchild
was a baby girl who was to be called Valérie. Martine, who
had not expected to have her baby for another ten days, had
begun her labour pains while her mother was unhurriedly
driving to Paris. Lily was vexed that nature had upset the
carefully arranged time-table. She told us that all the doctors,
including her own doctor husband, had been certain there
was no hurry. Dr Lehérissey, our retired village doctor, who
joined us every morning on the *plage*, and who at the age of
eighty looked rather like a wizened Buddhist priest, smiled
in a wise way.

'You see', he said gravely, 'that your modern specialists
are just as fallible as a modest country doctor like myself.
There's only one way of being certain of the exact date and
that is by having a Caesarian.'

Little Natalie told us that she had gone to the haberdasher's to buy her new niece a pair of knitted baby shoes.
Being an aunt at the age of four and a half called for certain
responsibilities! Just to make her position clear she enumerated her family. Her nephew Landry was France's baby
son; Charlotte, a niece, was Martine's first little girl, while
Valérie, who had just come into the world, was her second
niece.

This did not prevent her from asking me gravely for news
of the high-heeled shoes I had promised to buy her at
market. As the others were not in the secret, her question

made them smile but they did not like to hurt her feelings. I told her that she would have to wait till Friday, which was market-day. Dealers would then arrive from all over the countryside.

Patsy now made her appearance with various members of her house party. Jacques, she said, had bought a boat, a largish boat with a cabin to sleep four, but it was at Cherbourg and he would have to take possession of it there and sail it to Deauville where it would be moored in the yacht harbour. The news caused considerable excitement. We were full of admiration, though not precisely jealous. Sailing was a pastime we had never thought about.

Montauzan, partly because of Mrs Owen's illness, was not large enough this year to accommodate all the Gaudins, whose talents, musical and theatrical, helped to make the house such enormous fun. Jacqueline's brother, Daniel, the actor, who was married to the beautiful Natalie (we must not confuse her with little Natalie Durville), was therefore obliged to look elsewhere. My mother's friend, Mme Javault, came to the rescue. They went to lodge at her place. The family was growing at a great pace. There were now four children, the youngest of which was an infant.

Natalie, who could not have been anything else but a ballet dancer, wore a dress she had made out of a Negress's loin-cloth she had bought at Dakar. It was when she and her husband were on their way back from Madagascar where they had been with a repertory company, giving plays by Molière and Beaumarchais. Her long black hair hung loosely down her back. She was incredibly maternal and, to the stupefaction of the children in our set who had never seen such a thing before, she proceeded to breast-feed her baby. They were much more interested in this than in the latest Telstar or the twin Russian sputniks.

Her husband Daniel declared: 'I've never seen a baby's bottle in the house. All our children were brought up in this way.'

Little Natalie Durville was thrilled by Natalie Gaudin's baby. The little girl of four and a half was already the woman of tomorrow.

When the season gets going market-day in our village is quite a sight. The farmers' wives bring in their produce: cream, butter, eggs, cheese, flowers and vegetables. The fishwives bring the night's catch from Trouville, and from Roubaix and Tourcoing come materials for dresses and furnishing. Even the main street is lined with stalls. The hot Midi sends us its early fruit, Nantes its biscuits, and the shoe stalls are full of beach sandals.

As I made my way through the holiday crowds I met Mado Duprez and Annette Laurent. Annette was looking for black sandals. I told them that I was searching for mules with high heels for little Natalie.

'You're joking!' they said, laughing.

'No,' I answered. 'A promise is a promise.'

When at last I discovered a pair I took the precious parcel to the Durvilles' villa. Natalie was out, but Lily, her mother, quickly undid the wrapping and, seeing the contents, cried out: 'What beauties! Natalie has been dreaming about these. Let's go and look for her!'

We went to the grocery store where Mme Baudon told us that Natalie had just left. A few moments later we saw her coming out of the baker's shop.

'Look what Mme Henrey has brought you!' cried Lily.

The little girl gave one long, loving look at the shoes, and a moment later her tiny arms were round my neck. What a reward! What a wonderful day for me! As I had parked my car in front of the haberdashery shop we used it as a changing-room to try on the shoes.

'I'm going to wear them right away!' said Natalie.

Later on my way down to the sands I came upon Lily with her eldest daughter France, whose baby boy Landry was in a pram being pushed proudly along by Natalie wearing her high heels. She already had a blister but happiness made light of the pain. Lily in white was so astoundingly *chic* that she took my breath away. She seemed not a year older than her daughter. The holiday season was now at its peak. All the bathing-tents were hired out, the parasols allotted to the various summer residents. Dr Lehérissey, who disliked noise, deplored the loud-speakers which kept blaring out such diverse information as the finding of lost children, a cinema show on the beach or a twist competition.

Most of the smart set of the summer residents went back to their villas to lunch almost as formally as their forbears did in Edwardian times. I seldom troubled to go home for lunch, but stayed alone on the sands watching the spirited antics of the children from the holiday camps or the sudden invasion of our beach by sightseers, who arrived by coach from as far away as Germany and Italy.

On this particular day Fifille and I found outselves surrounded by a great wave of dark-skinned children. They were quite beautiful, but when I asked one or two of them their age they did not seem to know. There appeared to be as many girls as boys. One little girl, with an ebony skin and great lustrous eyes, told me her name.

'Are you on holiday with your parents?' I asked.

'No,' she answered softly. 'We are all foundlings.'

She wore pink briefs and a pink bra and, kneeling down in the sand, passed a brown hand through Fifille's fur.

A little boy stood watching her, not daring to do the same.

'That's my little friend,' she said. 'He wets his bed.'

The smaller child looked at me thoughtfully with big eyes under huge lashes, seeking in my features some reaction to this important revelation.

'Oh!' I exclaimed, and then laughed.

The little one came a step or two closer and then began to laugh too but very softly.

Soon a dozen children were squatting round me, playing with Fifille. Wondering who was in charge of them, I noticed a very fat woman with her very fat husband seated some yards away on deck-chairs. From time to time they would put down the newspapers they were reading to look in our direction.

'That's the cook and her husband,' said the older girl. 'In the afternoon they give us bread and chocolate, but the one in charge is the tall girl over there.'

About an hour later when the Durvilles came back from lunch Natalie came running up. She and one of the girls exchanged greetings.

'Do you know each other?' I asked, surprised.

Natalie answered with dignity. 'They are my friends. It was I who discovered them.'

'Yes,' said Lily, 'Natalie seems at her happiest amongst all these ebony heads—she used always to want to play alone.'

Lily had begun to tell me about her new grand-daughter when our colony of foundlings suddenly broke into an uproar. A tall lad had started a fight, and all the little ones went to the help of the one who was getting the worst of it. The girl who had been described to me as being in charge came over and separated them. She then smartly boxed the ears of the tall lad, who slunk away behind a coloured parasol and started to sob. My heart went out to him, for what is more pathetic than to see a child crying and to know that he has neither father nor mother to comfort him? Never would loving arms tighten round him. I was in the throes of these emotions when the lad sprang up, wiped away his tears and with a proud laugh rejoined his companions. A moment later he was laughing with the rest of them.

Lily, whose only defect was chain smoking, wanting to light up but finding that none of us had a lighter or a match, looked round with hungry eyes to see where she could find a light. Finally she went over to a young man to ask if she could light her cigarette from his. He rose politely and obliged her. On her return Natalie left her little dark-skinned companions to come over to our group and ask anxiously of her mother: 'Mother, why did you go to talk to that strange young man? You didn't know him, did you?'

Mothers and daughters! Daughters and mothers! What strange, adorable complexes this relationship entails.

9

EARLY in August M. le Curé, as his predecessors had always done, organized a village fair. My husband, who had been in Paris, spent the week-end at the farm before returning to London, and we went to the fair together, mostly so that I could buy a bracelet of melon seeds from little Natalie Durville, and thus keep a promise I had made to her some days earlier on the sands. At first she intended to make one of those long *sautoirs* that Mlle Chanel had brought back into fashion, but at the end of a whole afternoon she had only threaded enough seeds, by then rather grubby, to go round my wrist. But I told her that she might consider it bespoke, and that as soon as I arrived at the fair I would make my way to the stall presided over by Mado Duprez and her daughter Martine. Here also were Natalie's sister Sophie, Martine's cousin Estelle, and Caroline Laurent. Whereas Mado and the older girls were grouped behind the counter, Natalie had perforce to stand in front of it, for she was so small that she would not otherwise have been visible. However, she was radiant with happiness and self-importance. The bracelet of melon seeds held a conspicuous place on the table.

'I hope it isn't sold?' I said to Natalie.

'No,' she answered. 'I was waiting for you.'

I gave her my small contribution, telling her to give it to Mado who stood, looking rather like a sculpture by Praxiteles, behind the till. But the request appeared to puzzle her, for this was doubtless the first time in her life that she found herself acting as an intermediary. She had given me the bracelet for which I had given her in exchange a nice clean note. Why was she expected to hand it over to somebody else? This was indeed a puzzle for a little girl of four and a half.

My husband and I took her by the hand along a neighbouring avenue where there were sideshows under the trees. We saw young rabbits in a pen, and from time to time they were let loose in a toy village. The façade of each cardboard house had a number on it, and when a rabbit in search of lettuce leaves walked into a house whose number coincided with the one on your ticket the rabbit was yours. We bought several tickets for Natalie, but to her chagrin no rabbit walked into the house whose number she had drawn, and she was left to puzzle out another of those problems which appear so complicated to a child: why, if we had bought her so many tickets, did she have to go away without a rabbit?

The weather broke the next day and there was a severe storm. In the evening I drove my husband to Deauville whence he was flying back to London. On my return to the farmhouse I felt more than usually anxious. Neither my transistor nor television could keep my mind off his journey. He had once nearly been killed on such a trip. I had a quick meal at the corner of the kitchen table, but when I went to wash up I found that there was no hot water. There was no cold water either. The fear of a major mishap began to trouble me. As the water in the taps came from our own deep well, and as anything going wrong in the electrical system could disorganize the house and prove costly to repair, I was apt to panic. At midnight, however, my husband rang through from London, and at the sound of his voice I felt immediately better. As soon as I put the receiver down, I filled a bucket with hot rain water from the Aga and scrubbed the kitchen floor. The exterior of the house and some of the upstairs rooms were being repainted and men had passed in and out with their muddy shoes all day. I told myself that while I slept the kitchen floor would dry and all would be clean for the morning. I also prepared the feed for my four hens. I had a horror of left-overs and gave them everything that had not been eaten during the day.

The next morning, however, when I went out very early into the courtyard, I noticed that the stable doors were wide open. Fear seized me. My four hens had been stolen. A thief had broken in either during the night or soon after dawn. The perches were, of course, empty and there was no sign of the birds. I wept bitterly. These things can assume immense proportions when one is alone in the country. I had grown to love my hens, and I felt that I owed them a special affection because of the dastardly way in which I had behaved to their sisters.

Though the doctor had forbidden me to drink coffee, I put a generous amount in the earthenware percolator, and soon the kitchen began to smell good. I needed courage. I knew that I must telephone the *gendarmerie* about the hens, but first I rang Massard, the electrician, about the lack of water in the taps. To increase my feeling of unhappiness, I was suffering from the effects of a thorn from a rose tree which had embedded itself into the ball of my right foot.

At first I had taken the pain to be rheumatic and had done nothing about it. When I suddenly discovered that it was due to a thorn, I stoically removed the thorn with cuticle pincers, but the wound swelled badly. Brigitte then told me the story of a farmer who lived somewhere between Dozulé and Douville. He and his wife had just bought a few acres of land, and had been doing well when the man cut himself while trying to extract a corn on his big toe. He spent the day in jackboots bringing in the harvest. The toe was a bit

sore in the evening, but he bathed it and it felt better. The
next day it was not quite so good, and by the end of the
week he had to call a doctor. Gangrene had set in. They
amputated his leg and now, said Brigitte, he was in danger
of losing his hip.

'They'll un-hip him!' said Brigitte with an air of triumph.

This story terrified me. I opened a bottle of French
iodine which is twice as strong as the English variety and
poured it into the wound I had made with the cuticle
pincers. It burned the whole area.

When Massard arrived he said there must be something
wrong with the transformer on the main road to Caen,
because our neighbours, the Poulins, were also without
electric power.

'Be careful not to switch your television on,' warned
Massard.

As soon as he had gone I boiled some water for my
injured foot. My heroism with the extra strong iodine had
reduced the swelling and the pain had gone. I put on a
bandage and went to inspect the rose trees in the garden,
where the storm had given everything a miserable, blown
appearance.

Suddenly looking over the fence I saw my four hens
strutting across the orchard!

So it was the high wind that had wrenched the stable
doors open, and my hens, seeing the morning sun, had
merely taken advantage of the open doors to go off in
search of adventure. This time I wept for joy. Then, on
returning to the house, I became aware that the electric
motors were humming. Water would be coming up from
the well. There would be hot water in the taps. My house
was alive again. Even the painters were arriving with their
ladders and their pots of white and chocolate brown paint
for the half-timbering outside. I could smell their French
cigarettes and hear the low hum of their conversation. I felt

wonderfully happy. My foot was healing. The four hens were safe. My husband would be leaving the flat to begin a new day in London. God be praised!

The next morning all signs of the storm had passed, and I settled down again into that gentle monotony which had done so much to calm my mind since my mother's death. I almost sought solitude. I was not even sure to what extent I could bear the noise and agitation of visitors in my house. On Sunday morning after a peaceful week Georgette and Brigitte came together to bring the milk and some carrots from Georgette's garden, but as I was listening to a sermon on the radio I told them to take a basket and fill it with cooking apples, the first of the season. We could then divide them between us so that both Georgette and I could make apple tarts for lunch. Most of the apples at Berlequet were bitter cider apples and too small to cook, whereas over the years I had planted a great many eating apples round my house. Twenty minutes later Georgette and her daughter came back with the basket filled to the brim.

We decided that I should take Brigitte down to the village to buy the bread after which we could spend an hour on the sands. Her mother insisted that she must first be taken back to Berlequet to be made to look her Sunday best. Half an hour later I saw Brigitte bicycling down the orchard. I put the carrots with some onions that David had brought me into the slow cooking oven af the Aga. We then closed up the house, locked Brigitte's new bicycle up in the cottage and set off in the Citroën. When we reached the *plage* the tide was going out and already there was a great stretch of sand. Martine Duprez and her cousin Estelle Mathieu were sunbathing under a coloured parasol. They told us that Sophie Durville had gone to the Isle of Levant with her parents to tan under a Mediterranean sun. She was excited at going there but broken-hearted at leaving her Normandy friends. Martine Duprez, Estelle Mathieu and Caroline Laurent had been Sophie's inseparables this summer.

Patsy and Jacques had not yet succeeded in bringing their boat over from Cherbourg. One week-end when they had gone to fetch it a gale sprang up and they had to come back in the car. On another occasion the sea had been calm enough but there was a mist. All these false starts had made Lily Durville, before going to the Isle of Levant, exclaim with her rather caustic wit: 'You must rechristen it the Phantom Ship!'

Brigitte and I, too young and too old for Martine and Estelle, squatted on the sands to play 'pebbles'. This was a game that Matilda had invented when I was Brigitte's age, but in those days we played it with dried haricot beans instead of with pebbles. The art of the game was to hide in one's hand a number of pebbles or beans. The other players would guess how many one had. If they guessed correctly they seized the lot. If not they had to pay out the difference. Matilda, on her return from Versailles after the war, had taught it to Bobby and they used to play it interminably while walking home from the village with the provisions. Brigitte and I were now carrying on the tradition.

Suddenly little Natalie Durville came running towards us.

'Oh, Brigitte,' she exclaimed, putting out a hand to touch the new cotton frock Brigitte was wearing, 'how can you be so beautiful?'

Brigitte did not dare answer but she blushed with pleasure. Natalie, though so much younger, intimidated her. The fact that Natalie had such an elegant mother, two such beautiful married sisters, and another sister, Sophie, who was already so very sophisticated, impressed Brigitte enormously. Natalie tried to play 'pebbles', with us but she wasn't very good at counting yet and quickly tired of the game. So she ran off to play with a group of children of her own age. From time to time she would come back, stroke Brigitte's dress and again exclaim upon its beauty. Suddenly her features lit up with understanding. Brigitte was wearing the dress because it was the day people called Sunday. People were apt to look quite different on Sunday. Some of them went to church. Sophie went to church. But mostly Sunday must have something to do with dressing differently. Tara, the Dutch girl, who was with the Durville family *au pair*, looking after little Natalie, was lying full length on a gaily coloured towel reading a detective story. She looked like an odalisque. From time to time she would raise her eyes from her book and smile at us. Naturally beautiful, she took considerable care to keep herself so, and there was never anything that one could criticize about her appearance. She planned when twenty-two to become an air hostess with K.L.M., and it required but the smallest imagination to picture her in the tight-fitting coat and skirt and smart cap that would then be her uniform. Just now her skin was burned by the sun to the golden brown of a ripe plum.

'Tara,' cried Natalie, 'look what a pretty dress Brigitte is wearing. Today is Sunday!'

'So it is!' said Tara.

A question took shape in my mind, perhaps because of the sermon I had been listening to on the radio and I said to Tara: 'I suppose you're not a Roman Catholic! I should think that being Dutch you're more likely to be Protestant?'

Tara looked up from her book but did not answer.

What surprised me about her was that though she was strikingly beautiful, perfectly turned out, expertly made up, her hair carefully tended, she so often appeared to be alone. I at all events did not see bevies of boys chasing this lovely butterfly, but she was not the only one to remain distant. Many of the prettiest girls on the beach were to be seen either alone or with other girls of their own age. Beach flirtations were at all events not noticeable. The very expression 'to flirt' had an old-fashioned sound about it. And if the girls seemed happiest when they were together, the boys often gave the impression of preferring amusements of their own, the young ones roaring off on Vespas.

As August came to an end our orchards became strewn with copper-coloured leaves. Blackberries and hazel-nuts abounded in the hedges; apples and pears ripened. A circle of windfalls was to be seen at the foot of every tree, like a meal on a table waiting for the guests.

Annette Laurent's daughter, Caroline, was going as a boarder this autumn to the convent of the Sacred Heart at Brunoy, and one day I found Annette knitting a navy-blue jumper to be worn by her daughter over a light blouse. School uniforms, she pointed out, were now extremely becoming, and Caroline's blouses were made of nylon so that she could wash them easily. There was a revulsion, she said, against hideous school uniforms. But this was of recent date. Natalie Gaudin, the ballet dancer, complained bitterly of the horrors she had been made to wear at a very exclusive school for officers' daughters.

'Thick woollen underwear and black stockings!' she grimaced. 'But when I came home for the holidays and persuaded my parents to let me wear pretty nylon slips and fifteen-denier stockings my school clothes got their revenge. I nearly froze!'

Annette Laurent's husband, Michel, was connected with an American pharmaceutical concern, and his situation was considered an enviable one. The young couple had a splendid apartment in a good part of Paris.

'All the rooms face south and have balconies!' cried Annette joyfully. 'To the young married women in our set, a fine apartment in Paris is more desirable than diamonds or a pearl necklace. But life in Paris gets more expensive every day,' she complained. 'We spend every penny my husband earns. Of course, we have a wonderful time, lots of friends and parties every night. I really feel in the swim but we find it impossible to put money aside.'

She told us what her husband gave her every month to keep house and the sum was so large that I made her repeat it, thinking that I must have misunderstood her. No wonder the English were apt to look poor when they came to the Continent. Annette's chief complaint was that she could not yet afford to dress at Chanel or Balenciaga. She and Michel would also have liked to take the three children to winter sports. But that was out of the question. A week at an hotel for five people was unthinkable. If it had not been for this villa by the seaside, which had belonged to Michel's parents, the question of holidays would have been difficult indeed. I inquired about clothes for the children. Did these prove a heavy item?

'Quite heavy,' she answered, 'but I manage to buy nearly all their clothes with what I get from the Government every month in the way of Family Allowances.'

All our young mothers on the *plage* looked forward to the cheques they received regularly from the State and which were, I think, much more generous than in any other country. The more children a mother had the more money she drew, and what made it so enjoyable was that the husband's salary or her own private fortune had nothing to do with the case. Her status of mother was sufficient to entitle her to money of her own so that she was not dependent for her basic needs on her husband's whims. The *Familiale*, as the Family Allowances were called, made life very agreeable for our young mothers and gave them a sense of importance. They were not obliged to say 'Thank you' to their husbands, and in this respect they enjoyed while staying at home the same feeling of independence as a career girl who collects her wage packet at the end of the week. It made being a young mother much more fun. A thing like this, I reflected, might if it had existed in her time have changed the whole of my mother's character. She would certainly have felt less embittered with life.

There was another young mother in our set called Andrée Pradeau who had five young children, one of them a little boy called François, who at the age of seven was in love with Anne Poirot, Patsy's daughter of exactly the same age.

Andrée lived at 'Bois Lurette', a picturesque, rambling house in a fine park, whose former stables and coachmen's quarters had been converted into a separate establishment called Montauzan where the Poirots lived. Bernheim, the celebrated Paris picture dealer and a very wealthy man, had once owned 'Bois Lurette', and it had been his practice at the end of the last century to invite here Boudin, Pissarro, Claude Monet and Degas. He would say to them, so the story goes: 'Since your business is to paint, I pray you, sir, paint! Don't waste a moment. Here you have everything you need: apple trees, old farmhouses, beautiful sands and no material considerations. Stay as long as you like.' So they set to work and Bernheim bought many of their canvases with the result that in due course the astute picture dealer added considerably to his splendid collection of painting by French Impressionists.

Bernheim spent much of the 1914–18 war at 'Bois Lurette'. By that time he was an old man and had a delicate stomach. The house parties, the great receptions, the music and the dancing, the hospitality to artists, were over. Boudin and Pissarro were dead, while Degas would not see the end of the war. A little girl called Charlotte, who helped the postwoman to deliver the war-time mail, was given the special assignment of taking Bernheim's letters and his Paris newspaper, which also came by post, directly to his house.

In those days, as indeed now, the postman had a big round to do before arriving, sometimes in the afternoon, at the outlying farms. Every morning the old gentleman would wait for her at the top of the long avenue of noble cedars, and she was struck by the fact that even in the heat of summer he would be wearing a thick woollen dressing-gown. In her eyes he was not only a venerable figure but also a most benevolent one who, because of his delicate stomach, made her a present of all his bread tickets!

'Alas, my poor child,' he would say, 'I have come to the age when I can only eat rusks.'

Bernheim by now has gone to join the painters who have immortalized our Normandy coast. The Germans in the Second World War cut down the cedars that got in the way of their gun sights. Fortunately the park is still a noble one, and there are trees, says Andrée, which Boudin and Monet helped to plant.

I had first seen Andrée one winter's night during the 'phoney' phase of the war. Snow covered the orchards and fear was in our hearts. Andrée was still a girl—Andrée Salmont she was then—and, accompanied by her brother Bernard, an extremely handsome young man who loved the trees of 'Bois Lurette', had knocked at my door, having seen the light of the oil lamp in the living-room. That was in the days before we had electricity. They had been looking for my farmers to give them some message about their eldest boy who was serving his apprenticeship in a neighbouring village. We asked them into the house—this brother and sister in all their youthful beauty. My mother was there with my infant son.

A picture of that winter's night has stayed in my memory.

Their mother was an American who, when she married their father, Dr Salmont, was told by her own mother: 'If you marry a Frenchman you will bring tragedy into your life. There will always be wars in Europe.'

After that cold winter came spring and the German break-through. My husband came over and we fled with my mother and the baby in front of the advancing Germans. But, as I have said, we were obliged to leave my mother at St Malo to find her long dispirited way alone first to Paris and then to Versailles. The girl and the boy who had knocked at our door fared less well, so did the mother, who was arrested and taken to a concentration camp in spite of her American birth. When she was finally released it was to learn that her good-looking son had been seized and brutally murdered by the Germans. As for the grandmother, who had such good reason to fear wars in Europe, her own fate was no less terrible. On her way to come and live with her daughter in France, she was literally scalped in a motor-car accident and died after an operation.

Here now was Andrée Pradeau giving a tea party at 'Bois Lurette' with her youngest child just learning to walk. She had called him Bernard after her brother. She and Patsy were proud of their babies, more exquisite and more precious because they had the quality of autumn roses.

Annette Laurent and Natalie Gaudin arrived and soon the talk was about children. The ghosts of the past stood aside to allow the young mothers to discuss the present and the future. Annette Laurent had plans for staying with rich friends in the Midi, friends who were rich enough to have servants and a yacht. She voiced, I think, the general opinion, which was that a holiday in a house where there were servants might prove something of a dream holiday. There were times when we all felt that there was too much work to do.

'When my husband and I were quite newly married', she said, 'we were happy to stay every week-end in Paris. The streets were animated, the theatres were all open and there were amusing restaurants to explore. But now as more people own cars the restaurants tend to close on Saturday and Sunday. Every car one buys goes faster, and I become increasingly nervous. I admit it can be fun to pile the luggage and the children into the car and go off for the week-end, but then there's the unpacking at the other end and the repacking to come home. By Monday I'm exhausted, and by Friday, when I have more or less recovered, it's time to begin all over again. The week-end in the country that started as something to look forward to becomes in the end a burdensome task.'

To this Natalie Gaudin answered: 'Daniel and I have always known that. So we never bought a car. What we do we like to do in the simplest way. We try to live near whatever theatre Daniel happens to be playing at, and after the evening performance, when the children are in bed and fast asleep, Daniel and I go out by ourselves. Generally I go to meet him at the stage door and we go off through the streets on foot.'

'Yes,' said Annette, laughing, 'but you two are artists, theatre folk. You succeed in combining two different lives. We are not all as fortunate.'

My son, who had come to join me at the farm, had not yet been to see Matilda's grave in the little churchyard at Auberville. He had not been with me a week before he told me how much he missed her. He even remarked one evening that since her death the old farmhouse no longer had any charm. He said: 'Every time one walked into the house, she was in the kitchen waiting. Then too she admired me. In her eyes I was somebody important. Whatever I said amused her prodigiously. It was easy to make her laugh. She would laugh till the tears trickled down her cheeks. Have you any idea how wonderful it is to have somebody who never blames and never criticizes? I shall never have that again as long as I live. Parents intimidate one. It isn't their fault but even *you* treat me as if I were only half grown up.'

Granny for my son was gentleness, comprehension, admiration. Dear little Granny with her still golden hair, those twisted, deformed fingers which stuck out at all angles like the half-timbering in front of the house, knobbly and old and friendly. He loved her soft accent of the Loire and her keen intelligence. Her death had robbed him of something vital, a whole segment of his life.

His words upset me terribly. Was I, his mother, therefore of so little importance? Of such small account that the house no longer had any charm? I fled to hide my tears. Had not her death robbed me also of a whole slice of my life, leaving me a daughter without a mother, the mother of a son who though loving me (I hoped, even felt sure) tenderly, did not consider me as the gentle one, the understanding one, the admiring one?

The next morning was one of those hot September mornings when the world was at its best. The bees were busy in the garden and swarmed round the hole by my bedroom window. The hive would become my inspiration. I must work like the bees to show my gratitude to heaven. I would embroider something, a tablecloth, so as to have long hours of quiet meditation. The sun shone, the grass was lush and full of fallen apples and pears, the bees made music and my four hens were scratching vigorously for insects on the other side of the garden fence. Their favourite spot was the giant pear tree now heavy with small hard fruit from which farmers liked to make *poiret* or pear brandy, whose potency was immense. M. Javault's fig tree, which his wife had first brought to us as a spindly cutting, and which we had planted in a large blue tub outside Matilda's window, was now proving that it was not barren but capable of producing good fruit—to be exact, two robust figs nearly ripe enough to pick and eat. Life was eternal, and something vigorous like M. Javault's fig tree was always telling us so. My garden was also afire with dahlias and asters from the plants that I bought at Dozulé that sad Tuesday morning when I went officially to record the purchase of the piece of ground at Auberville. My mother's grave cost me exactly the price of a single tube of cortisone!

10

NATALIE GAUDIN came out of the sea with water shining on her long dark hair which she wore plaited, like a native Tahitan girl. She had entrusted me with the care of her rings, for she was such a strong swimmer that she feared to lose them in the water. Her supple body, trained to dance since early childhood, made her an expert at the crawl and she was a joy to watch. Her baby was at my side in the carry cot, her other children were making sand castles with companions of their own age. This, said Natalie, was the most delightful moment of the day, the moment of relaxation after her swim.

'We have already booked Mme Javault's cottage for next year,' she announced as she sat down beside me and put her rings on again. 'We hope to stay longer and mother will be joining us.'

Her mother had been prevented from doing so this year because she was looking after a charming aunt of eighty-five.

'The poor darling has outlived her contemporaries,' said Natalie. 'As a girl she was so exquisitely beautiful that she received no fewer than thirty proposals of marriage. She refused them all laughingly but firmly because, so the story goes, she was afraid of men. The thirtieth proposal coincided with her thirtieth birthday. Her friends felt certain that on this occasion she would prove less difficult, but the young man was not so young as the previous ones had been. Also he had a beard which was beginning to turn from dark

to pepper and salt so she felt no compunction about turning this one down too. The idea of remaining unmarried
never worried her and her gaiety made her many friends.'

Natalie went on: 'You will like my mother. Like Joan of
Arc she comes from Lorraine. She was an officer's daughter.
Most of the men in my mother's family were soldiers. Metz
where they lived is a garrison town.

'I sometimes wonder what made me want to dance.
Fortunately my parents made no objection. My mother was
both spirited and pious. We all of us are. When my mother
reached the age of fifty-five she decided to go off on a series
of pilgrimages. She wanted to visit all the holy places in
Italy, but as this promised to take a considerable time and
cost a good deal of money she bought a second-hand
bicycle, the oldest and cheapest she could find, and to save
hotel bills spent her nights in the cemetery of whatever
town or village she happened to be visiting.

'She told me', Natalie went on, 'that it was very inspiring
to go to sleep propped up against a tombstone surrounded
by cypresses and with the sky full of stars above. She said
that if it rained, which it seldom did, there was nearly always
a family vault to shelter in and that it was wonderful to wake
up in the morning with the birds singing, the sun streaming
down and the melodious sound of water from a nearby
fountain. There was always a fountain, she said, where she
could bathe her face and refresh herself unobserved.

'She was away for over six months and came back to us
looking ten years younger. She had even cut her hair short.
The stories of her many pilgrimages delighted us. Our
rather Bohemian life enchants her, and when she stays with
us in Paris her affection for Daniel makes her want to
protect him from the noise of the children. She thinks he
must be tired after the theatre, and she invents all sorts of
devices to procure him peace and rest. Daniel tells me
laughingly that her efforts to coddle him are far more

disturbing than the noise of the children to which he is accustomed. But mother's ideas are engrained in her. She says that it's a man's privilege to remain from time to time undisturbed. Officers' daughters were taught in her youth that the warrior's rest is sacred!'

What did Natalie plan for her own future? Did her role of mother preclude her from fresh triumphs in the theatre?

'No,' she said, 'I am a born optimist. I only notice what is good in life. That doesn't mean that I have no sorrows or disappointments but I do my best not to dwell on them. Next year when I have finished breast-feeding Cyrille, my baby, I shall ask mother to look after the children and I shall go back to the theatre. Perhaps I shall get a wonderful part in a play that will run for at least two years. Who can tell? But today here I lie on the sands sunning myself. Tomorrow a girl friend, who is also on the stage, is taking me back to Paris in her car. I shall enjoy myself immensely. I shall sit beside her while she drives and we'll talk about the theatre and the amorous adventures of all our friends. We will put all the children at the back and hope that some of them at least will sleep all the way. I do hope the baby won't be ill. Then there will be the excitement of going back to my Paris apartment and taking a stroll after supper along the Boulevard St Germain.'

So Natalie Gaudin went back to Paris and soon the last of the summer residents would have gone. The *plage* would be deserted and we would be busy picking the cider apples. But suddenly Lily and her husband Jacques Durville came back from the Île de Levant with their daughter Sophie, and though their stay would be short, it was as if we had been granted a reprieve. Little Natalie was so pleased to see her parents and her sister again that she behaved almost like a spoilt child.

But as I say this visit gave us a few more days on the sands, and on Sunday morning, rather to our surprise, Gaston Duprez came to join us. Gaston, tall, slim and very good-looking, though born in the village, had the distinction of a Parisian man about town. In manner he was distantly courteous and his suits were impeccably cut. He was the equivalent of the village squire, and his beautiful wife, Mado, entertained very elegantly at 'Le Plein Air', their house on the road to Caen, which was quite a show place.

Gaston sat down rather gingerly on the dry sand beside his father-in-law, Dr Lehérissey. He it was who, as a young doctor, had brought Gaston into the world. He wore a dark suit and his trousers were beautifully creased. He could never understand why we liked to get wet in the sea and then come and dry ourselves in the sun. Mme Lehérissey, the doctor's wife, who for all her womanly gossip had an astute financial brain, had brought her tapestry. She had throughout a long life covered all the chairs and most of the walls in her husband's consulting-room with her work.

'Every year I decide to give it up,' she said. 'Then I start another piece and hurry like mad to finish it. By the way, that reminds me'—the sequence of her thought was not clear—'I put on a stew of haricot beans and I mustn't let it burn!'

She put her tapestry away and went as far as the bathing-tent. A few moments later we saw her in conversation with a young women whose hair was tinted such a strange colour that one might have supposed she was wearing a hat. Gaston looked critically at the stranger and said: 'I presume that my mother-in-law has met a tenant.'

Mme Lehérissey, though conversant with statistics appertaining to the Bourse, had also most widely invested her savings in nice little villas conveniently situated along the coast, and these she rented out at a modest profit every

summer. But the holidays were over now and Mme Lehérissey's tenants were doubtless, one by one, giving back their
keys.

At the twelfth-century church of Auberville a young
priest attached to a children's holiday camp was celebrating
the last Mass of the season. Before driving out there my son
and I picked the loveliest roses in the garden to put on
Granny's grave.

The church was filled with September sunshine. A young
mother who sat beside us had brought her baby, but the
baby cried so much that his mother was obliged to go out
and walk up and down between the tombstones during all
the rest of the service. The baby's cries reached us from
outside and became mingled with the voice of the young
priest. I also cried but my tears were muted. Three months
had passed since Matilda had lain here in her shining oak
coffin. Now brown leaves were falling from the trees and
the gardens were filled with asters and dahlias.

After the service we saw the mayor of Auberville standing at the foot of his wife's grave. He turned to greet us and
said: '*Bonjour*, Mme Henrey, you will see that your Mama's
grave is beginning to sink in. I advise you to ask your
farmer to bring some good earth and heap it on. Thus you
will be spared the pain of seeing it subside. A grave that
subsides is a sad thing to see. You will need to wait a full
year before you put a headstone.'

Three months had passed and three new graves had been
dug since Granny was laid to rest.

I had said to Gaston that morning when he came to the
plage: 'Now that my house has been repainted, won't you
honour me with a visit?' And as whisky had become the

fashionable drink in France, I told him that I would do my best to prove an adequate hostess by offering him some.

Gaston answered: 'I hate whisky but I have a great desire to see how you have arranged your little house.'

I also invited Lily and Jacques Durville.

But as it happened David Owen arrived first. He had formed a habit of looking in at tea time on Sundays, always dressed for the occasion in grey flannel trousers, a blazer and a beret. Like so many Englishmen abroad he couldn't get used to an afternoon without tea and cakes. So chiefly in his honour I always put out a schoolroom tea in the kitchen on Sunday afternoons.

Gaston and Mado arrived while David was helping himself to bread and butter and jam.

'Ah,' said Gaston, 'tea! And bread and butter and jam! That's what I should like. And greengage jam, if I'm not mistaken!' He served Mado and himself, and exclaimed: 'Home-made jam! What we in France call *confiture de bonne femme*. People don't trouble to make it any more. But this is unusually good. Who made it?'

I had put out the last pot of Matilda's greengage jam. She had made it the previous summer when we had such an exceptional crop of plums of every kind that the birds and the wasps left them uneaten on the trees. Last year had been a greengage summer. But I was not here to see it. I had left for London just before they ripened.

Now Lily and Jacques Durville arrived and we made fresh tea. My guests did not hide their delight. Everything was wonderful, they said. I felt flattered but I tried not to show my pleasure. They inspected the house, the great stone fireplaces, the half-timbered bedrooms. A beautiful house, they said. A fairy-tale house.

'But', said Gaston, as we came back to the kitchen, 'you should pull down the wall that divides the kitchen from the living-room so that you throw into relief the double stone fireplace which is the whole beauty of the house. You need to give it more air and space.'

Jacques Durville said: 'What you really need to do is to put the kitchen somewhere else. I'm sure it's wrong for it to be here. As it is now, you will always be tempted to sit in it, and you will neglect the other rooms, which are so lovely, Now, if I were the owner of the house . . .'

How right I had been not to allow my happiness to show. Gaston had put into words what I had often felt myself. The wall should be knocked down. Jacques Durville's criticism was equally sound. We did tend to neglect the other rooms. I felt like saying: *Touché!* But I also felt a little sad. A different house would not be my house. I would not find Matilda's presence in it any more.

I took them to their waiting cars. Did I look a little crest-fallen? Mado took me aside and said: 'Your house is a darling house. Don't dream of altering it.'

The two cars drove off, Mado and Gaston in one, Lily and Jacques in the other. The orchard became suddenly very quiet.

Villers-sur-Mer,
Calvados.

January 1963.